LOCAL TRAVEL GUIDE TO NORTH MACEDONIA

JOANA TRAJANOVA

OPPIAN

Published by Oppian Press
Helsinki, Finland

ISBN 978-951-877-186-2

CONTENTS

WELCOME TO NORTH MACEDONIA

MACEDONIA – NOW OFFICIALLY KNOWN AS NORTH MACEDONIA –WAS part of SFR Yugoslavia until 1991 when the county gained it's independence. The country is located in Southeastern Europe, north of Greece.

North Macedonia has a total area of 25,713 km2 (9,928 sq mi), with some 748 km (465 mi) of boundaries, shared with Serbia to the North, Kosovo to the northwest, Bulgaria to the east, Greece to the south, and Albania to the west.

Although North Macedonia does not have a coastline, believe me when I say that this small country is definitely worth visiting. Well Macedonia is home to a range of interesting sights and things for tourists from landscapes, to historical and cultural landmarks. There's the "Pearl of Macedonia" in the gorgeous Lake Ohrid, to the rugged hills outside Prilep. The country has plenty of gripping historical sites, like Heraclea Lyncestis or its numerous medieval fortresses. Then there's all the wonderful cultural insights you're able to find, from the tobacco production in Prilep, to countless bazaars, to the intriguing remnants of its communist past. Macedonia has plenty to offer those who choose to visit it. As the proverb says if you want to have the best experience in some country, ask the locals and go to the places that are most recommend by themselves.

While most of the tourists usually pay a visit to N. Macedonia during the biggest Christian holidays, and they are mostly visiting only the capital city Skopje and Ohrid, an antic city with great historic value, the country has beautiful views during all year-round and some of them can be only seen during specific season.

Tourists usually fall in love with the idyllic small villages the way some people live their lives. The locals are typically friendly, and the food is fantastic. At the same time, the culture is a mix of Macedonian, Albanian, Turkish, and Mediterranean influences, which makes this small country even more appealing.

This country really is quite low-key and it's only by visiting Macedonia that you get a chance to find out what a fun, intriguing place it is.I think in part why so few people tend to travel to Macedonia, is that it simply hasn't been put on their radar.

As we all know planing a trip or a vacation may be very exhausting, so hopefully this travel guide will save you many worries and make the whole experience more pleasant

Climate

North Macedonia stands at the junction of two main climatic zones, the Mediterranean and the continental. Periodically, air breaks through mountain barriers to the north and south, bringing dramatically contrasting weather patterns; one example is the cold northerly wind known as the *Vardarec*. Overall, there is a moderate continental climate: temperatures average in the low 30s F (about 0 °C) in January and rise to the high 60s and 70s F (about 20–25 °C) in July. Annual precipitation is relatively light, between about 20 and 28 inches (about 500 and 700 mm). Rainfalls of less than 1 inch (25.4

mm) in the driest months (July–August) rise to nearly 4 inches (about 100 mm) in October–November. Because of differences in local aspect and relief, there may be considerable variation in the climate, the eastern areas tending to have milder winters and hotter, drier summers and the western (more mountainous) regions having more severe winters.

Official Language

The country has two official languages: Macedonian and Albanian. Both languages are spoken in the capital and in cities where a minority of Albanian-Macedonian people live (mostly in Western North Macedonia), while in southeastern North Macedonia people speak only Macedonian.

Of course your stay in the country would be much more easier if you would know a few words in Macedonian of Albanian language and locals would appreciate your effort.

The people are kind and helpful, and most of them have at least basic knowledge of the English – language, so if you find yourself in some kind of trouble don't hesitate to ask locals for help.

Official Currency

Also, an important point in your visit is the currency, although the official currency is the Macedonian Denar (mkd) most of the places accept euros too. But it is preferable if before traveling you have some cash in North Macedonian currency, because there are places that only accept mkd like local markets and supermarkets too.

Where to exchange money?

You can change money at banks, official exchange offices or even at the airport (just sometimes the Macedonian Denar may be a bit cheaper to buy at the airport). Also you can just get Macedonian Denar from ATM machines. Make sure your debit card company knows you will be using the card in North Macedonia and make sure you have a 4-digit PIN. Take a couple of hundred dollars (or Euros) with you in case there's some trouble that needs to be sorted out.

1euro = ~62mkd

Currently in use are coins of 1, 2 , 5, 10, 50 denars and notes of 10, 50, 100. 200, 500, 1000 and 2000 denars.

Most of the banks work from Monday to Friday 8:00-16:00, and on Saturday 9:00-13:00. Some of them may work to 17:00 or 18:00.

ATM's are almost on every corner, and credit and debit cards, such as Visa Electron and MasterCard are accepted everywhere, in restaurants, hotels, bars, shops etc. North Macedonia is one of the cheapest country to visit on the Balkan Peninsula if not the cheapest. My advice is to pay in denars rather than in dollars or euros.

Safety and unwritten rules

The criminal rate in North Macedonia is quite low. There are no random attacks and no sexual harassment on the streets. Also, on 29th June N. Macedonia had its first Pride Parade with absolutely no violence, so it is good to say that the whole nation is accepting the homosexual relationships and there are some laws that protect homosexual people in the country. There are many LGBT+ organizations, who take care that none of these laws are being violated.

Also, it is not allowed to go naked or topless on the public beaches, of course in some private beaches it is not forbidden or in some isolated beaches.

It is preferable if you are in the capital to travel with public transport i.e city-bus transport. It will be cheaper for you and definitely you will get to know better the city. However take care of your belongings and always put them in a safe place.

Always convert the asked price in denars to euros or your currency, that way you will not get cheated on and you will not be overcharged.

Emergency numbers and assistance

Fire brigade +389 193

Police +389 192

Ambulance +389 194

AMSM – telelphone for road condition and information +389 2 15555

AMSM – telelphone for roadside assistance and towage +389 196

TRAVELING TO NORTH MACEDONIA

The Republic of Macedonia is not part of the European Union, nor is it part of the **Schengen Area** that allows free movement between countries, something many EU countries currently benefit from. If you are from an EU member country, valid passport is all that's needed to visit up to 15 days visa free.

Visitors to North Macedonia must obtain a visa from one of the North Macedonian diplomatic missions unless they come from one of the visa exempt countries.

Registrations of foreigner

All foreign citizens – irrelevant whether a visa is necessary for their entry in the Republic of North Macedonia or not – are obliged to register themselves in the nearest police station **within 24 hours** of their entry on Macedonian territory.

Although if you are staying in a hotel / hostel, they will do that for you automatically once you check in the hotel. You get a little card ("Potvrda" = "Attestation") that says when you arrived and when you left. Keep it. In theory, someone might ask to see it when you leave.

6

It's not waterproof though, so be careful! Failure to register is €1000 penalty.

Which country's citizens do not need visa to enter North Macedonia?

Citizens of the European Union and of the countries signatories to the Schengen Agreement can enter with just a valid officially issued ID card or a passport. The visa free stay for EU citizens is 90 days.

The traveler must:

- Hold a passport valid at least six months on entry with one blank visa page
- Hold proof of sufficient funds
- Hold proof of onward/return flights
- Hold all documents required for the next destination

Currency restrictions for enter:

10,000 Euros or equivalent must be declared.

Currency restrictions for exit:

10,000 Euros or equivalent must be declared.

How to get to North Macedonia?

The county has two international air traffic airports – the first one is located near the capital and it is called Skopje International Airport and the second one is in Ohrid, practically on the apposite side of the country. The airport in Ohrid is called St. Paul the Apostle.

Skopje International Airport

The airport is situated only 23 km (20 min with a car) from the capital city – Skopje.

The runway at the Skopje Airport encompasses runway 2,450 m long and 45 m wide, system of taxiways and platform with 15 stands for all types of aircraft, starting from the general aviation up to B747 and AN 124.

St. Paul the Apostle Airport

The runway at the Ohrid Airport is 2,550m long and 45m wide, which has 13 stands for the aircraft of the general aviation to the TU 154 aircraft.

The airport is 9 km away from the city – Ohrid. The location of the airport makes it perfect if your trip is going to take place in the southwest, west N. Macedonia. In that way you will not just spend precious time on traveling.

Getting Around

As expected, Skopje, Ohrid, Strumica and Bitola have the most connections. Bus fares are dirt cheap running between 3-15€ depending on distance. Also a common way of getting around is in taxis in most of the cities the taxi service does not overpass 2€, by this I mean in the city limits from one place to another. You could find taxis usually waiting near by the bus stations, so finding one wouldn't be a problem. Many taxi companies have their own mobile apps, you could reserve / order one online. Besides free ordering, the apps have numerous advantages over "classical order ". Its functionality provides comfort and ease of use. Ordering via internet will save your money spent on phone call, locate button will allow easy retrieval of addresses. The option of monitoring arrival of the vehicle in real time will help you better planning of time while you wait.

Taxi Navigators

Strumica has its two city taxi apps named **City Cab Strumica 1588** and **Radio Taxi Strumica 15 – 87**. In addition are the numbers of popular taxi companies in Strumica 13 188, 13 098, 15 060, 13 870, 13991.

Skopje has multiple city taxi apps, from which one of the most known is **Global Taxi Skopje.**

Bitola – **Taxi Tea Bitola**

Kicevo – **Vase Taxi Kicevo**

Veles - **Taxi Perka Veles**

Prilep – **Taxi 5 Prilep**

Vikni Taksi – Викни Такси is a standard taxi navigator app which contains all of the numbers of existing taxi companies in the country.

All of the named apps are available on Google's Play Store and Apple's App Store.

Airport *TAXI Services*

Skopje Airport offers taxi transfers from Skopje to Skopje airport Alexander the Great, Ohrid, Bitola, Thessaloniki, Chalkidiki, Athens, Sofia, Belgrade, Prishtina and all other towns in Macedonia, Greece, Bulgaria, Serbia, Montenegro, Albania, Kosovo, Slovenia, Croatia, Italy, everywhere across Europe and further. The drivers will pick you up with a name card from any location convenient for you and drop you off to the desired destination.

Car rental agencies

. . .

MIDA Rent-a-car

'MIDA Rent a Car (MIDA), located within the premises of Skopje "Alexander The Great" Airport and headquartered in "Business Center MIDA" in Skopje, is one of the best rent a car companies in Macedonia. As a proud rent a car booking leader MIDA Rent a Car offers a variety of transfer services in and around Skopje, as well as any location in Macedonia, including shuttle transfers for small groups and large families, or private transfers for couples and single travelers.

Inter ways rent-a-car

Addresses:

Skopje downtown Main Office

Bul. Ilindenska 97 Skopje, Macedonia

Open: Monday-Saturday 9am-5pm

Office at Skopje (SKP) Airport

Main Terminal Building / Arrival Area

Open: Monday-Sunday 24/7

Office at Ohrid (OHD) Airport

Main Terminal Building / Arrival Area

Ohrid City

Meet & Greet service(free delivery/pick up)

Skopje Main Office Contact

. . .

(+389) 2 3062 484

(+389) 75 40 40 30

contact@interways.com.mk

Skopje Airport Contact

(+389) 2 2563 313

(+389) 76 420 444

airport@interways.com.mk

Ohrid Contact

(+389) 75 40 40 31

ohrid@interways.com.mk

Website: https://macedoniarentacar.com.mk/

More than 150 vehicles available, all new and clean. Prices start from 13 EUR per day

Hertz Car Hire

Address: str. Skupi no. 8, Skopje 1000

Hours: Monday – Friday: 8:30 am – 4:30 pm

Saturday: 9 am – 2 pm

Sunday: closed

Phone: 02 313 4391

Relax Rent a Car Skopje

Address: No. 16-2/4B.C Skopje 1000

Open: 24/7

Phone: 071/ 392 488

Website: http://www.macedonia-car-rental.com/index.php

RENTAL RATES

All rates are in EURO.

Daily rates are for 24 hours from start of rental. If a daily period is exceeded by more than 1-3 hours will be charged as per 1/2 day. More than 3 hours will be charged as per full day.

Weekend rate starts from 12:00 PM on Friday until 10:00 AM on Monday.

Mounth rate is valid for 30 days.

Minimum rental period is 24 hours.

Rates included:

- unlimited mileage.

- third party liability insurance higher level (T.P.L.), according to the government regulations.

- theft protection (T.P.).

- collision and damage waiver (C.D.W.), covers renter's responsibility for damages of the rented vehicle with the exemptions of:

- damages on the tires not caused by fire or accident;

- driving under influence of alcohol or drugs;

- written statement by police is not presented at the time of check-out;

All the same whether CDW was accepted or not, a charge of 500 euro will be applied, in the event of theft of the car.

METHODS OF PAYMENT

We accept credit cards as follows VISA, Eurocard/Mastercard. Cash payment - any convertible currency or the equivalent in Macedonia denars. DEPOSIT and total cost of rental is required at the beginning of the rental.

DELIVERY AND COLLECTION

Skopje capital – free of charge – in work time.

Skopje airport – free of charge – in work time.

Any location in Macedonia – after speaking with our staff.

GASOLINE

Gasoline consumption is payable by the renter. If the vehicle is returned with less fuel then rented, the customer is charged for refilling the tank.

EQUIPMENT

Map, ski rack, and snow chains. All the equipment are free of charge.

CROSS BORDER POLICY

In the case when the customer intends to use the rented car abroad MD rent-a-car must be informed previously. If the customer will drive the car outside of the country he has to notify MD Rent and to pay additional insurance.

. . .

Avis Car Rental

Address: Mito Hadzivasilev-Jasmin, Skopje 1000

Hours: Monday – Saturday: 9am – 6 pm

Sunday: Closed

Phone: 02 322 2046

Websites: https://www.avis.co.za/drive-avis/car-hire-locations/europe/macedonia

https://rental24h.com/macedonia/skopje-airport/avis

Parking zones Skopje

The parking zones are organized in 4 zones according to the location, the distance from the city center and the duration. The four zones are as follows:

- 1. First zone- The Red Zone 1 (A) - it is in the very center of the city where you can only park for two hours. After that you must remove your car from the parking lot.
- 2. Second zone- The Yellow Zone 2 (B) - it is near to the center of the city, next to Hotel Bristol and Business Center Mavrovka. The parking time limit is 4 hours.
- 3. Third zone- The Green Zone 3 (C) - It is in the Neighborhood Debar Maalo and the Complex MTV, Macedonian Academy of Science and Arts and the Court Palace. There is no parking time limit.
- 4. Fourth zone- The White Zone 4 (D) - it is in the Municipality of Aerodrom and there is no parking time limit.

How to pay?

When you park your car on one of the parking zones you can pay by:

- **SMS**:

- To start the parking: Send SMS to 144 144. The text message must include the parking zone number and the car license number:

„Zone number space car license number"

Ex. Acceptable: A3 SK1234AB

Ex. Unacceptable: A3 SK-1234-AB

After you send the message please wait until you get return message: „"Your car SK1234AB is parked in zone A3 until 12:00", which is correct message and you will be properly charged.

IMPORTANT! Do not leave the parking lot until you get the return message and check if you have received it. If you receive return message: "Your car SK1234AB is not parked in zone A3", please contact the call center of the Public Enterprise City Parking- Skopje. Otherwise, the Public Enterprise City Parking- Skopje does not take on responsibility.

- To stop the parking: send SMS to 144 144 with text: "S"

Text messages with text: "STOP", "END", etc. are not acceptable!

After you send SMS, please wait until you receive return message:

"Parking stopped on 25.01.2014 at 12:30. Parking fee: 45 MKD"

The SMS fee is according to the price list of your mobile operator.

You must send SMS only from Macedonian pre-paid or post-paid number.

- **With parking ticket i.e. scratch card**

If you decide to regulate your parking with parking ticket, all you have to do is:

- Go to the nearest store and buy your parking ticket.

- Scratch the circles proper to your minutes, hours, date and month of parking.

- Place the ticket on the windscreen of your car.

IMPORTANT!

The ticket must be placed on the windscreen to be clearly visible.

Otherwise, not displaying or irregular use of the parking ticket is subject to sanctions prone to the "Decision on Public Parking Lots" (advertised in Official Gazette of Republic of Macedonia, No. 17/8)

When the user has not paid the parking fee is subject to sanctions i.e. clamping in force, prone to the "Decision on Public Parking Lots" (advertised in Official Gazette of Republic of Macedonia, No. 17/8).

SKOPJE

Skopje is the capital of the Republic of North Macedonia, in the center of the Balkan Peninsula. Over time it has experienced Roman, Byzantine and Ottoman rule. Skopje is thousands of years old and bears the burden of a turbulent history. At the same time it is a modern capital that offers rich cultural and natural attractions and an outstanding experience of a typical Balkan life.

The city is surrounded by several mountain ranges: Skopska Crna Gora to the north, Vodno and Jakupica to the south. The river divides the city into a southern and a northern part. The 15th-century Stone Bridge (Kamen Most) connects the Ottoman Old Bazaar (Stara Charshija) on the Vardar River' s north bank with Macedonia Square and a statue of Alexander the Great to the south.

Skopje is home to the world's fifth biggest cross, in the 66-meter high Millennium Cross, built to mark 2,000 years of Christianity in North Macedonia. It sits atop Vodno Mountain in the city and can be reached by cable car or by foot.

Except for the Old Bazaar you will not find any other old monuments in Skopje, because of the catastrophic earthquake that hit the city in 1963. As a result of the earthquake a major part of the city center was ruined which later were redesigned by the Japanese architect Kenzo Tange. Experts say that some of the best brutalist architecture is located in Skopje.

Getting around Skopje

Walking is your best option as all the Skopje attractions are fairly close to each other. However if you want to take a tour throw the city or you are just too lazy to walk, I will suggest to use public transportation. Until recently it was possible to just buy the ticket from the driver but now you need to get a special card, called Skopska (karticka) card. It costs 150 mkd for the card and you already have some credit on it, one-way bus journey within the city costs 30 mkd. You can get the card in newsstand booths.

Where to stay?

- Hotel Senigallia

Situated in the very city center of Skopje and with a boat-like design, Hotel Senigallia is a 3-minute walk away from Stone Bridge and from Macedonia Square. Guests can enjoy the on-site bar and 2 open terraces by the river Vardar. Kale Fortress is 600 m from Hotel Senigallia, while the lift for Millennium Cross is 5 km from the property. The nearest airport is Skopje Alexander the Great International Airport, 24 km from Hotel Senigallia. This property is also rated for the best value in Skopje! Guests are getting more for their money when compared to other properties in this city.

- Hotel De KOKA

Opened in April 2014, Hotel De Koka offers a restaurant, elegant rooms, free WiFi access and free private parking. Guests can start their day with breakfast every morning, get groceries in a shop 100 m away or buy snacks in a mini-market in the hotel. The Skopje Train Station is located 1.6 km from the property and the Alexander The Great Airport is located 20 km away. An airport shuttle can be arranged for at surcharge.

- Hotel Arka

Situated in the historic nucleus of the Old Bazaar of Skopje, Hotel Arka offers modern accommodation with a panoramic bar and a rooftop terrace available at any hour for a drink. The reception desk offers tour guides services and assists with booking ballet and theatre tickets. Hotel Arka is set a 10 minutes walking distance to the Central Square. In the same area you can enjoy various entertainment and dining options. Skopje Bus and Train Station can be reached within a 5-minute drive, while Skopje Airport can be found within a 25-minute drive.

- Skopje Marriott Hotel

The hotel is set in Skopje, 100 m from Macedonia Square and 200 from Stone Bridge. It offers a spa center with an indoor pool and facilities such as hot tub, massage and steam room.

You will find free WiFi and a 24-hour front desk at the hotel. Kale Fortress is 800 m from the hotel and Skopje City Museum is 650 m away. The nearest airport is Skopje International Airport, 24 km from Skopje Marriott Hotel.

Where to go, and what to visit?

Church of St. Clement of Ohrid

To understand the struggle and history of Macedonia, and its people you have to learn about St Clement. This unusual Orthodox Church is an architecture gems. The buildings were composed with 4 globes shape, one sits on the top act like a cupola and the other three as a main building. And if the church need to send out the impression of a grandeur, it wouldn't get much better than walking into the cathedral through a high striking arch from a dreary street to greet with all golden painted array of iconographies and one of the biggest chandelier in Skopje. It is located only a few minutes walk from the Macedonia Square.

Usually weddings and baptisms going on. You won't be interrupting if you are respectful, and those rites in themselves are just extraordinary! This may not have the most icons or the oldest, but it's worth a visit!

Holy Savior Church

This church is between the entrance to the Kale fortress and the old bazaar area, and is entered through a door to a courtyard which does not indicate what is inside. It does not look like a church because during the Otoman empire, while churches were tolerated they could not be visible from outside, therefore this church is partly underground and has no spire or tower. Entry cost MKD 100. A tiny church set in a quiet courtyard with breathtaking icons and beautiful wood carvings. A real little treat. Also can sit in the cool interior and contemplate the surrounds. The tomb of Goce Delcev, Macedonia's famous freedom fighter is preserved in the church.

Memorial house of Mother Theresa

This museum, a modern construction based on Mother Teresa's birth house and built on the site of the church in which Anjeze Gonxhe Bojaxhiu was baptized, gives a concise account of the history of Mother Teresa from her birth, to her times in Ireland and India, to her award of the Nobel Peace Prize and her beatification as Saint Teresa of Calcutta. Simple photos, testimonies and artifacts paint a simple picture of a simple lady whose impact was immense. There are at least 3 life sized statues of her inside and outside the museum. There is a multi media amphitheater in the basement, a shop on the ground floor and a wonderful, small chapel on the second floor above the gallery – a very modern design of glass and metal with filigree dove and fish symbols of the catholic church.

Outside near the river is the outline of the house she used to live in. The house was destroyed in an earthquake.

Skopje ZOO

While in Skopje it's highly recommended destination for you and your kids. So many to see varieties of birds, wild life animals, tigers, lions and lionesses, monkeys, elephants, jaguars, hippos, alligator, sea lion, reptile section, eagles and many more to be seen. Also there are three coffee shops one at the very entrance of the zoo and the one in the middle, you can have your refreshments and even pizza while the little one play in a safe playground area. The last coffee shop is just over looking the pond with the ducks it is great for the hot summer days. The price is 50 MKD(about 1€) per person and up to 3 or 4 years is free. Also the kids can ride a pony horse and go on a ZOO tour with a guide.

KALE FORTRESS

Located in the old town of Skopje this fortress has stood watch over Skopje since the 6th century. It was built of stone blocks from the ruins of the city of Scupi, during the rule of the Byzantium Emperor Justinijan the 1st.

During Ottoman occupation Kale Fortress was partially destroyed. Today only 121 meters of the wall remain intact, along with three watchtowers and several historical findings from past archaeological excavations. The walls are well worth the climb for great views of the city and what the guards were able to see when it was the key to the defense of the area.

Address: Samoilova, Skopje 1000

Phone: 02 312 9323

Working Hours: Mon – Sun, 08:00 – 19:00 (8:00 am – 7:00 pm)

Entrance: free of charge

Old Bazaar

Located only a few minutes from the city's Kale fortress, Skopje's old bazaar is second largest bazaar in the Balkans after Istanbul and it surely has the orient charm. You can easily get lost in the maze of narrow streets, wandering around and enjoying the incredible views of this extraordinary place. There are numerous craftsman shops selling everything from copperware to traditional Macedonian folk costumes. There are also traditional restaurants and coffee houses throughout selling kebab, lahmajdun (meat pie), and Turkish delight.

In the Old Bazaar is located the hotel Arka which has one of the most beautiful views in town. You will have the view of the old bazaar just in front of you.

Mustafa Pasha Mosque

The Ottoman-era structure stands on a plateau above the old bazaar, built in 1492 by Mustafa Pasha

The mosque is largely intact from its original state, and no additions have been made through the years. The body of the daughter of Mustafa Pasha is buried in the turbe next to the mosque. The mosque has a rose garden.

Monuments in Square Makedonija

Many of the classical-looking buildings, statues and monuments which were built in Skopje happened during the controversial "Skopje 2014" project.

With three major street converge the square Macedonia is Skopje's central square and heart of the city. In the center of the square there is a *fountain* featuring the most popular Macedonian warrior *Alexander the Great on his horse Bucephalus.*

Also there is a *statue of Mother Theresa* which can be found on

23

Macedonia Street, near the Memorial Museum for Mother Theresa. She was born in Skopje from Albanian parents.

Two statues dedicated to him has the Macedonian *revolutionary Goce Delcev* too. One on Macedonia Square and one in the City park. His tomb can be found at the *Church of St Spas in Skopje*. You'll recognize his statue by his prominent mustache.

Another extraordinary building is the triumphal arch called *Porta Macedonia* on Pella Square is dedicated to 20 years of Macedonian independence and was erected as part of the Skopje 2014 project. Inside there is a souvenir shop.

Opposite to the City Museum of Skopje is a *statue* to commemorate the devastating *earthquake* of July 26 1963, that killed over 1000 people and made more than 100,000 people homeless.

Krste Petkov Misirkov is the writer of the famous work "On Macedonian Matters". His *statue* can be found at Pella Square, close to the GTC (Shopping Center).

In 2011 a statue of *Justinian I* was placed at Macedonia Square near the Stone Bridge. Justinian I is commonly known as Justinian the Great and was an Eastern Roman Emperor from 527-565. His birthplace was near Skopje.

The *statue* of one of the founders of the Macedonian Revolutionary Organization, *Dame Gruev* is placed on Macedonia Square next to the Stone Bridge.

These are only a few of the many monuments that can be found in Skopje's center, almost all of them represent an important period of the country's development.

Skopje Aqueduct

Just outside the city you can find the *Skopje Aqueduct* – the only surviving aqueduct in Macedonia. It dates back to the 1st century, when it was used to supply water to the Roman colony of Skupi. Later it was used by the Byzantines and Ottomans for the same purpose. Note that the aqueduct will not be easy to find if you are planning to drive yourself. It is best to go with a guide.

MNT Macedonian National Theater

The theater is luxuriously decorated, with glided ornaments inside and outside and statues on the roof. The new building which meets the highest standards for construction of such institutions, offers possibility for nourishing the art, culture and realizing high-quality performances.

Macedonian National Theatre is the oldest and largest theatre in Republic of Macedonia founded in 1945. Since its founding, the theatre team has staged nearly 300 premieres and the theatre troupe has given over 8,000 performances. It is aiming to establish and profile its own repertoire as well as aesthetic concepts by which it shall distinguish itself from the other theatres in Macedonia and at the same time promote itself as a national theatre institution.

Youth Cultural Center (MKC)

Cultural institution, based in Skopje that organizes more than 200 different cultural events per year - performances, exhibitions, promotions, workshops, concerts, debates and film screenings. YCC also organizes four of the most important festivals in Macedonia

The bohemian part of Skopje

In some 15 minutes away from the center you will find Debar Maalo, one of the most exclusive ones in the city because of the location. The most famous and beautiful street there is so – called the Bohemian Street. There you will find numerous cafes, restaurants and kafana – s. You may ask what a kafana is? Well it is a nice relaxed place, where during the evening hours is played old music (starogradska muzika). However Debar Maalo is not as busy as the Center of city, so you can find your time of peace too.

MATKA CANYON

Matka Canyon is a popular area for the capitals residents to escape the city and head to the hills for some adventure as well as those backpacking the Balkans.

A gorge in which a rich complex of mediaeval building survives, including churches, monasteries and remnants of a fortress (the mediaeval town of Matka).There are dozens of caves and large number of endemic plants and animals. The Canyon covers an area of around 5.000ha and is located 15km south-west of Skopje. It is also important to mention that there are 77 species of Balkan endemic small butterflies in area of Matka Canyon, while 18 other species are new to the science. The Treska canyon is vertically cut into the massive of Suva Mountain. The different formations in the canyon like the karrens, flutes, valleys, cracks, crevices and caves have been formed by a long term impact of the mountain rivers, as well as by great temperature oscillations. In the surroundings of the Treska Canyon one can find dozens of caves, the most beautiful ones being Vrelo, Krshtalna and Ubava.

.   .   .

What to do?

- **Exploring the caves hidden in Matka Canyon**

You can either rent a kayak and paddle for 1.5 hrs to the cave or take a tourist ferry. The ferry takes around an hour and includes entrance to the cave and a tour of Matka Canyon.Price is 400 Denar each (£5.50 / $7.10)

The cave system is relatively small above the water but at the far end of the cave sits two perfectly still lakes reflecting like a mirror the amazing detail of above. The underwater sections of the Matka cave are some of the deepest in the world and still have yet to be fully explored.

- **Climbing in Matka**

The major climbing season in Matka begins in spring, round the Easter holidays when visitors come from countries from all over Europe. The season continues throughout summer and fall until the end of November.

- **Kayaking**

The Treska Canyon is also open for kayaking. You can rent out either a double or single sit on top kayaks from the start of the canyon. Rental is 200 Denars per hour (£2.77 / $3.50) per person but this is slightly cheaper for the double kayaks.

Where to stay?

Canyon Matka hotel and restaurant, founded in 1939, The Canyon Matka hotel resembles a sprawling, two-story chalet. All of the 10 rooms are decorated in local traditional decor with large windows and plenty of amenities.

Address: Str.1 nn Village Dolna Matka - Skopje, Republic of North Macedonia

Phone: +389 2 2052655

+389 78 503 000

Mail: info@canyonmatka.mk

Reception | Working hours: 08:00 – 24:00 CEST

Tips

- Be sure to bring with you a dry bag to keep your camera, wallet etc. dry
- Try to find out the time of the buses back and time it
- Wear some good shoes as the cave is slippery and muddy

BITOLA

Bitola is the second largest city in Macedonia with a history
dating back to the middle of the 4th century B.C. Back then it was
known to the ancient world as *Heraclea Lyncestis*, a city founded by
Phillip II of Macedon (father of Alexander the Great). For this, Bitola
is the oldest city in the Republic of Macedonia. Exploring Bitola by
foot is the easiest way to take in the city's sights and sounds. It takes
about a day to see the main sights such as the many mosques, markets,
and the Saat Kula 17th century Clock Tower.

Where to go, and what to visit?

Shirok Sokak

The place to see and be seen in Bitola. This pedestrian boulevard is
lined with shops, cafes, and restaurants. It begins in Magnolia Square,
Bitola's main square. From here you can already begin to see the old
Macedonian and Ottoman-style houses. Once you've seen the nearby

Saat Kula (Clock Tower) and Vergina Sun Fountain in Magnolia Square, start your stroll up Shirok Sokak Street.

Museum of Bitola

A great way to learn about the Balkan struggle for independence from the Ottomans. The museum itself is situated in a mid-19th century building that served as a military academy. In 1983 it was repurposed into a museum to honor its most famous student, Mustafa Kemal Atatürk, a Turkish army officer and first President of Turkey. The Museum of Bitola also houses archaeological exhibits, reproductions of Leonardo Da Vinci, ethnographic materials such as traditional costumes, a reproduction of a traditional village home, and the Exhibition Hall of Mustafa Kemal Atatürk that contains examples of his written work, memorabilia from his private life, as well as battle strategies and a library.

Ruins of Heraclea Lyncestis

Heraclea Lyncestis was an ancient city in the kingdom of Macedon. Phillip II of Macedon founded it in the 4th century B.C. The ruins themselves are located just 2 kilometers south from the center Bitola, at the foot of Baba Mountain. Though smaller than the original city, the archaeological site of Heraclea Lyncestis holds several important buildings and sites. These include the Roman theatre, Roman thermae (bath complex), small and large basilicas added by the Byzantines, Jewish temple, and intricate church floor mosaics that are fantastic examples of early Christian art.

Ishak Çelebi Mosque

Popularly known as Ishakkiye, this mosque was named after its founder, Judge Ishak Çelebi. The 16th century mosque is the largest in Bitola, located along the north bank of the Dragor river. In its spacious yard are several tombs, attractive because of the soft, molded shapes of the sarcophagi.

Bitola's Old Bazaar

Although much smaler that Skopje's Old Bazaar, is one of the city's most important cultural and social features. Walking the cobblestone streets it is easy to gain a sense of how the bazaar felt in its glory days – it boasted over 900 shops selling everything from housewares to farm animals. Historically, the Old Bazaar was the place where you could find anything you needed (soap, cobbler, silk, gunpowder, wool, leather, etc.). Nowadays the bazaar is still a lively place for shopping, especially for souvenirs.

Saat Kula – Clock Tower

With an imposing height of 32 meters, is the most recognizable landmark of Bitola. Until 1912 the Clock Tower in Bitola measured the time according to "alla turca" and afterwards the modern measurement of time "alla franga" was introduced.

Set on a square base with sides of 5.8 meters, the Clock Tower is entered through a door on the north side, and a stone spiral staircase leads to the upper end of the tower, which houses the clock mechanism.

Museum of the Albanian alphabet

The "Congress of Manastir" aimed at standardizing the Albanian Alphabet, was held in Bitola (then Manastir) from November 14 to November 22, 1908.

Before the Congress in Bitola, the Albanian language was presented as a combination of six or more different alphabets, with numerous sub-variants. About fifty delegates from different parts of the Balkan Peninsula participated in the congress, of which thirty-two had the right to vote.Today, the date November 22 is celebrated as national holiday in Albania, Kosovo and Macedonia. The building in Bitola where the congress was held today is transformed into a museum.

The Museum of the Albanian Alphabet was opened on November 22, 2012, and in the reconstructed building are placed photographs, documents and wax figures that affirm the revival, cultural and advanced movements of the Albanian people.

Dzepane – the fortress above Bitola

Built in 1876, it consists of four unique buildings, built from carved stone and surrounded with high stone wall.

The object is located in the former Bitola barracks area and is considered to be the supreme architectural accomplishment of the masons from Smilevo village.

Especially interesting are the large number of lightning rods surrounding this building, as a different kind of protection, now against natural influences.

Deboj hammam in Bitola

It is assumed that it was probably built in the XVII / XVIII century, when it served as a hammam. It is located in the Old Bazaar, near the Haydar Kadi Mosque. This profane architecture is rich in architectural forms from the outside and plastic decoration that adorns numerous rooms inside.

Over the time the building was constantly damaged and repaired.

After the conservation and restoration the Deboj got its original appearance, with a beautiful façade, several small and two large domes that dominate over others.

Today the Deboj serves as closed bazaar, in which various different textile goods are sold.

Haydar Kadi Mosque

The mosque is located on the left side of Dragor River, near the former Sheep Market and still existing Deboj in Bitola. According to the preserved historical sources the mosque was built in 1561 – 62. The project was made by the famous Turkish architect Sinan Mimar.

Auto and Ethno Museum "Filip" in village Krklino

a private museum located in village Krklino, just 5 km from Bitola.

With collection of objects which in quality and quantity exceeds many state museums, Auto and Ethnology Museum "Filip" is a location you can't miss during your visit in Bitola.

The museum contains large collection of antique cars including: Simka Ariane from 1953, Opel Olimpija, Ford Taunus, Pezo404, Plimut Valijant, Moskvic, Opel Olimpija, Fiko, Folsvagen Buba, Citroen, twentyfour motorbikes six decades old in a great condition such as BMW, DKW, NSU, MAKS etc.

Ethno section of the museum contains a rich collection of objects, carefully arranged in several authentic rooms, such urban, village, Jewish and Turkish, as well as a collection of old costumes, instruments, weapons, household items and so on.

Auto and Ethno Museum " Filip" is a result of long and dedicated hard work of Boris Tanevski and his family.

Recently, toward the development of rural tourism in village Krklino, the museum is enriched with another activity, i.e. visitors can spend the night in an authentic room, as well they can taste a number of Macedonian specialties prepared in a traditional way.

Phone: Tel: +389 (0) 47286666

Mobile: +389 (0) 70312146

E-mail: info@muzejkrklino.mk

PLACES WORTH VISITING

Bukovo Monastery

Located in a beautiful mountain area near the villages Bukovo and Krstoar in Bitola region, was built in 1837, in 1845 the monastery had two monks and in 1865 there was only one abbot.

Today the monastery is maintained by the local population.

In the middle of the monastery is located the church and from the old monastic enclosure walls and the main gate, only small portion was preserved. The old monastery lodgings were built southwest of the church, and they were recently renovated.

Due to the proximity of city of Bitola, the clean air and water and the picturesque mountain scenery, the monastery today is one of the most visited sites for picnic near the city.

How to get to Bukovo Monastery?

Up to the monastery leads an asphalt road through the village Krstoar and "Krstoar Monastery" in length approximately 6 km (3.7 miles) from Bitola. Much of this road (4km) is paved and is in relatively good condition, up to Krstoar Monastery. The rest of the road with a length of 2 km is a dirt road, which is in relatively good condition.

Also the monastery can be reached by foot (~ 20 min) through Bukovo village up to which also leads an asphalt road.

The house of Karinte family on the Main street – Shirok sokak

Eleni Karinte was the Great Love of Mustafa Kemal Ataturk.Eleni was a Vlach and Christian girl from from a well known family with house on the Main Street – Shirok Sokak. Falling in love with a Turk (Muslim), was a big shame for her family, and according to the legend, she was sent to Lerin (Florina), where is lost every trace about her. Many people call Eleni Karinte and Mustafa Kemal the "Balkan Romeo and Juliet", and the house where she once lived, today is tourist attraction in Bitola.

Goce Delchev Memorial museum

The memorial museum dedicated to the famous visionary of the Macedonian Liberation Movement is located on the street Stevce Patakot No. 11 Bitola.

The opening of this museum is based on the occasion of the visit of Goce Delcev's visit to this house, to Bitola in 1901.

The exhibition consists of two halls, which cover an area of 37m2 of which the first hall houses items connected to the life and the revolutionary activity of this apostle of the Macedonian Liberation movement. As part of the exhibition, in an appropriate room, there is also a glass cabinet holding the symbols of the revolutionary oath of the Organization as well as the weapon of the Ilinden period. Also an important segment of this exhibition is the interior of the room in which Goce stayed and where meetings were held has been preserved and recreated with bringing authentic items of that time to show the original ambient of the rooms.

Big Lake Mountain Hut

Big Lake is a post-glacial lake on an altitude of 2218 m and one of the most attractive locations on Pelister National Park.

Near Big Lake is located "Big Lake" mountain hut, which with prior notice is open for tourists and visitors. The Mountain hut has six big sleeping rooms with a total of 30 beds and 20 mattresses. There is also one big dining room with a large capacity.

For every person who will choose to sleep in the hut, there are clean sheets, pillow, and woolen blankets.

Open hours:

From the beginning of May until late October the mountain hut is always open on weekends. (on demand on other days)

Phone: +389 75 458 782

E – mail: pnolev@gmail.com

Neolica Mountain Hut

The hut is located at an elevation of 1440 meters and has a capacity of 48 beds.

Starting from the center of village Lavci, up to the mountain hut leads marked mountain trail which is appropriate for all ages ~ 2 hours hiking.

.   .   .

House Bastion

Located in Bitola, 70 m from the centre, House Bastion provides 24-hour front desk and air-conditioned rooms. Free WiFi and free parking are available. A grocery shop can be found within 80 m. Various restaurants, cafes and bars are reachable within 100 m.

The Museum of Kemal Ataturk is 100 m away. The Old Town can be reached within 2 km. The Pelister Mountain is at a distance of 12 km.

Hotel Theatre

Centrally located in Bitola, in a quiet residential area, Hotel Theatre offers air-conditioned rooms with free WiFi. Free public parking is available on site and free private parking can be found 50 m away from the property. The main pedestrian street Shirok Sokak can be found within a 5-minute walk from the Hotel Theatre. Bitola Train Station is set 2 km away.

Hotel Bulevar

Hotel Bulevar features a garden, bar, a shared lounge and terrace in Bitola. Among the facilities of this property are a restaurant, a 24-hour front desk and a shared kitchen, along with free WiFi. The hotel has newspapers and a fax machine and photocopier that guests can use. Guests at Hotel Bulevar can enjoy a continental or a buffet breakfast. Florina is 34 km from the accommodation.

rices

What to do?

Hiking Tours

.   .   .

Pelister Eyes – Big and Small Lake Hiking trail

Hiking trail: Hotel Molika– Caparska Preseka – Hunter House – Small
Lake – Big Lake

- Track length:16 km
- Time: 8-9 hours (approx)
- Difficulty: Hard
- Track altitudes: 1420m – 1590 m– 2000 m – 2180 m –
  2220 m
- Begova cesma (hotel Molika) 1420 m
- Caparska presek 1590 m
- Hunter House 2000 m
- Small Lake 2180 m
- Big Lake (Mountain House, Dimitar Ilievski – Murato) 2218 m
- **Recommended for physically strong and
  experienced mount hikers.**

Kopanki – Jorgov Kamen – Hiking on Pelister

Hiking trail: Hotel Molika – Kopanki – Jorgov Kamen and back to
hotel Molika

- Trail length: 4 km
- Time: 2 -3 hours (approx)
- Difficulty: medium
- Track altitudes: 1420 m – 1610 m – 1744 m – 1610 m -1420m
- Begova cesma (hotel Molika)1420 m
- Kopanki 1610 m
- Jorgov Kamen 1744 m
- Kopank 1610 m
- Begova cesma (hotel Molika) 1420 m

- **Recommended for everyone**

Rounded Hiking trail: Hotel Molika– Peak Pelister – Hotel Molika

- Trail length: 21 km
- Time: 8,5 hours (approx)
- Difficulty: Very Hard
- Track altitudes: 1420 m – 1936 m – 2468 m – 2542m – 2601m
- Begova cesma (hotel Molika) 1420 m
- Mountain House Kopanki 1610 m
- Vanguard 1936 m
- Peak Stiv 2468 m
- Peak Ilinden 2542 m
- Peak Pelister 2601 m
- Marten rock 2000 m
- Caparska Preseka 1590 m
- Hotel Molina 1420 m

Recommended for physically strong and experienced mount hikers

Golema Livada – Hotel Molika – Hiking on Pelister

Trail to Golema Livada: Hotel Molika – Children Hostel – Mala Livada Golema Livada – Information Centre of National Park Pelister – Hotel Molika

- Track length: 6 km
- Time: 2-3 hours (approx)
- Difficulty: easy

- Track altitudes: 1420m – 1270 m – 1240 m – 1187 m – 1350 m – 1420 m
- Begova cesma (Hotel Molika) 1420 m
- Children hostel 1270 m
- Mala Livada 1240 m
- Golema Livada 1187 m
- Information Centre – National Park Pelister 1350 m
- Begova cesma (Hotel Molika) 1420 m
- **Recommended for everyone who visited Hotel Molika and National Park Pelister**

Palisnopje – Hotel Molika – Hiking Trail on Pelister National Park

Trail to Palisnopje: Hotel Molika – Tourist Information Centre – Palisnopje – Kopanki – Hotel Molika

- Track length: 7 km
- Time: 3 hours (approx)
- Difficulty: Easy
- Track altitudes: 1420m – 1350 m – 1400 m – 1610 m – 1420 m
- Begova cesma (hotel Molika) 1420 m
- Information Centre – National Park Pelister 1350 m
- Palisnopje 1500 m
- Kopanki 1610 m
- Begova cesma (Hotel Molika) 1420 m
- **Recommended for everyone who visited Hotel Molika and National Park Pelister**

Recommended equipment for hiking:

- Appropriate Footwear and Clothing
- Extra clothing selected according to the season
- Sunglasses with UV filter
- Sunscreen (SPF 30 – recommended)
- Personal First-aid allergy kit
- Nutrition (cereal bars, snack)
- Hydration (at least 1 water bottle)
- Insect repellent
- Walking poles

Jeep excursions in Bitola

First World War – Macedonian Front – one-day excursions in Mariovo region

Some of the decisive battles on the Macedonian front occurred in Mariovo region, which had serious consequences on the civilian population due to famine, diseases and military actions.

Today in Mariovo region there is large quantity of remains and memorabilia from that period, and many stories about the "struggle" of the civilian population during the war and in the postwar period.

This one-day educational excursion aims to convey these stories, but also offers you an unforgettable one-day experience through the picturesque landscapes of Mariovo – the least populated region in Macedonia.

Details:

- Type of tour: Jeep excursion / Jeep safari

- Pick up/drop of location: Bitola (hotel, parking lot,…)
- Difficulty: Easy, recommended for everyone
- Dates: On demand / spring, summer and autumn
- Duration:~ 8-10 hours
- Altitudes: Bitola 615 m, locality Lakite 1015 m

Program:

09.00 h – Departure from a previously agreed location in Bitola

- Short break near "Elevation 1050"
- Tourist drive through Municipality of Novaci
- Short break at a picturesque location near the village of Staravina
- Visit of trenches and bunkers in Staravina village
- Visit to the church of St. Demetrius in Gradeshnitsa village (XIV c.) The only object in this village that was not ruined during the war, although was directly hit by a grenade.
- Visit to the Zovich village, bunkers near the village and the private museum collection in the Ethno house "At the Bridge".
- Free activities (possibility of visiting the Movie Bridge near the village)
- ~ 16:00 – arrival in Bitola

Feel the nature – one-day jeep excursion to White River – Mariovo

In the upper part of this river there is absolutely no source of pollution, and the nearest city and industrial capacity are 70 km away. The locality "Lakite" is excellent picnic location and can be reached only with 4×4 vehicle.

If you are looking for escape from the urban chaos, then this forgotten place in Mariovo is the right choice for you.

Details:

- Type of tour: Jeep excursion / Jeep safari
- Pick up/drop of location: Bitola (hotel, parking lot,...)
- Difficulty: Easy, recommended for everyone
- Dates: On demand / spring, summer and autumn
- Duration:~ 8-10 hours
- Altitudes: Bitola 615 m, locality Lakite 1015 m

Program:

• 09.00 h – Departure from a previously agreed location in Bitola

• Tourist drive through Municipality of Novaci

• Short break at a picturesque location near the village of Staravina

• Tourist drive to the locality Lakite (arrival around 10.00 h)

• Leisure activities.

• 15:00 h – departure back to Bitola

• Visit to the monastery St. Athanasius near the village of Staravina

• ~ 17:00 – arrival in Bitola

Big Lake – Pelister – one day jeep excursions

According to the legend "Pelister Eyes" – the mountain lakes "Big" and "Small" on National Park Pelister – were formed from the tears of two sisters, who were in love with the same boy – Pelister. Their mother did not allow them to marry the boy and in anger sent them to the mountain, with a curse: to be close, but not to see each other. The daughters shed so many tears, from which two beautiful lakes were formed.

Located at an altitude of 2.218 meters (Big Lake) and 2.180 m (Small Lake) the "Pelister Eyes" are a great location for the nature lovers.

Details:

• Type of tour: Tourist drive – 4×4 Jeep taxi on demand – Jeep Safari

• Difficulty: Moderate

• Location: National Park Pelister

• Dates: May – November

• Duration: 8-10 hours (~ 3 hours driving in one direction)

• Altitudes: Bitola 615 m, Small Lake 2.180 m, Big Lake 2.218 m

Program:

• 08.00 – Departure from previously agreed location in Bitola

• Tourist ride through National Park Pelister with short stops on picturesque locations.

• Visit of the Small Lake (2.190 m)

• Visit of the Big Lake with opportunity to explore the beautiful scenery and landscapes, to breathe clean air, drink pure spring water or mountain tea in the mountain lodge (If it's open. It usually works every weekend).

Mariovo – Rural Adventure – one-day jeep excursions

Surrounded by high mountains, Mariovo is characteristic for its history, ethnology, traditions and culture. This Jeep excursion is a great opportunity to come in touch with the rich cultural and natural heritage of the least populated region in Macedonia.

Details:

• Type of tour: Jeep excursion / Jeep safari

• Pick up/drop of location: Bitola

• Difficulty: Easy, recommended for everyone

• Locations: Villages – Makovo, Rapesh, Staravina, Gradeshnica, Zovich

• Dates: On demand / all year

• Duration:~ 8-10 hours

• Altitudes: Bitola 615 m, Gradeshnica 800 m, Zovik 680 m

Program:

The departure is at 9:00 o'clock from previously agreed location in Bitola, followed by a tourist ride through the villages Logovardi, Novaci, Makovo and Rapesh in duration of about 40 minutes. Short break is planned at panoramic location near Rapesh village, where visitors will have opportunity to photograph the beautiful landscapes surrounding this village. Then we continue through the canyon of Crna River to monastery of St. Athanasius near village Staravina. This monastery is one of the few locations where you can have the whole Mariovo region at the palm of your hand. Excellent panoramic location, so don't forget to bring your camera. The church St. Demetrius (16th century), monastery St. Ilija and the remains of the Roman fort Pesta near village Gradeshnitsa are next stops and final stop is Zovich village with the famous Stone Bridge.

The excursion ends at 16:00, when we get back to Bitola (about 1 hour drive).

Upon request – traditional lunch at the Ethno House in village Zovik can be organized.

Tetovo

Located at the foot of the Shar Mountains which separate Macedonia from Albania, Tetovo has long been a stronghold of the country's ethnic Albanians. While the city is often known as the unofficial capital of the Albanians of North Macedonia, and expressions of Albanian national pride, in the form of flag waving from houses and cars and graffiti depicting the map of the "Greater Albania", are common, this is by no means an exclusively Albanian city, and referring to it as such will offend the non-Albanian residents, particularly the ethnic Macedonians. The style of dress is different and people speak a different language, so visiting Tetovo may be the most unique experience once you are in North Macedonia.

Where to stay?

Mercure

Situated in Tetovo, 20 km from Bitolska, Mercure Tetovo features air-conditioned accommodation and a bar. Among the facilities of this property are a restaurant, a 24-hour front desk and room service, along with free WiFi. The accommodation provides evening entertainment and a shared lounge. Guests at the accommodation can enjoy a continental breakfast.

Hotel Emka

Situated within 20 km of Bitolska, Hotel Emka in Tetovo has a number of amenities including a garden, a fitness center and a bar.

Among the facilities of this property are a restaurant, a 24-hour front desk and room service, along with free WiFi. The accommodation features a tour desk, luggage storage space and currency exchange for guests.

Hotel Lirak

Situated in the town's central Illyria Square, Hotel Lirak is the oldest hotel in Tetovo. It offers free WiFi and air-conditioned rooms. The on-site restaurant serves Macedonian and international dishes. Tetovo Bus Station is at a distance of 500 m. Skopje, the capital city of Macedonia, and Skopje International Airport are 35 km from the Lirak Hotel.

Trips to Popova Shapka, the popular ski resort on Shar Mountain, can be organized upon request.

Where to go, and what to visit?

Leshok Monastery

A monastery 8 km outside Tetovo, build in 1326 and is a beautiful example of splendid Byzantine architectural style. In its complex are the churches of St. Athanasius of Alexandria and the Holy Mother of God Church. The area around the village of Leshok is distinguished by a beautiful environment, pure mountain air and a magnificent view. The good climate makes it one of the most beautiful and healthiest places in North Macedonia.

Furthermore, the church has several beautiful frescoes which possess historical value and which originate from different periods. The most popular fresco is called "Judgment Day".

Many people come to Kiril Pejcinovik's grave in Leshok to bow and read "The epitaph" written on his tombstone. It is Pejcinovik's most famous and most meaningful piece which was written in the Leshok monastery and to this day, it remains a mark of recognition for all generations throughout Macedonia.

Mehmed Bey's Mansion

Build in an oriental style. From the first half of the 19th century, the Mehmed Bey's mansion is in the ownership of the Palloshi family. The building is in the centre of Tetovo, and represents a monumental structure together with the Painted mosque, the double Hamam, and Pasha's bridge over the Shkumbin river. The general architecture picture of the building represents a harmonious entity. All the areas are nicely furnished with doors and decorated ceilings. The consistence of this much variety demonstrates the wealth of the owners, and their huge families.

Painted Mosque

The painted mosque was built in 1495. This monument presents an artistic realization, with specific outside decoration, and especially in the inside. For centuries, this building preserves its religious function, as well as the education and cultural function. The building is distinguished for its great artistic values.

In its composition scheme it consists of a prayer room, hayat, minarets, mausoleums, drinking fountains; all of these surrounded by a large wall covered with tiles. The main entrance of the mosque is in the western side, but there are also two other entrances, one in the southwestern side, and the other in the northern side. The painted mosque in the inside has a square form; the prayer room has a unique volume and is covered with domes, which is lightened with 30 windows, 15 down and 15 up. What makes it more attractive is the decoration of the walls. The decorations of the interior and the exterior walls reflect geometrical motives interwoven with floral motives giving an outstanding value. The exterior: like the Sofa and the columns; the interior: balconies, mihrabs, domes, are all painted in the Secco technique.

The turbe, as a part of this structure, presents a characteristic example of the monument upon the tomb of the Ottoman period, built in the XVI century. It is of the type of open turbas.

Hamam of Tetovo

One of the landmarks of the city is the historic Hamam of Tetovo which sits on the right bank of the river. Dating from the 16th century, the building shows an Albanian influence on the typical Islamic style. It now hosts The Gallery of Visual Arts.

Arabati Baba Tekke Monastery

The dervish monastery began construction in 1538 under Sersem Ali Baba who taught there until his death that year. Afterwards, it was completed in 1548 by his last remaining pupil Arabati Baba, with Sersem's Turbe at its core. It's last renovation was performed by Redzep Pasha in the 18th century. The monastery was not only a religious institution, but also a cultural and educational one. The grounds are also quite lively with lots of trees and plants, making for a peaceful retreat from the world.

Ethno – museum

The smallest Ethnology-museum in the world, can be found in the house of the collector Simeon Zlatev-Mone. The museum has a fund of 1,150 items. Due to the limited space, the museum can host only one visitor. The largest part of the displayed materials date from the end of the 19th and the beginning of the 20th century, but there are also fragments of ceramic items, which are 5,000-8,000 years old.

Gostivar

There is one legend about the city, regarding the origin of the city's name. In the Middle Ages, the city was highly visited by guests from all over the country, and in the summer days a large trade gathering (fair) was traditionally held every year. Such a tradition continued during the Ottoman Empire. Due to the great visiting to the settlement by people from other parts, the Turks among themselves in Turkish, often called it "*gosti var*" (having guests). Then there were many inns in the city, so it is assumed that the "hospitable city" - "the city of guests" became - Gostivar. Volkashin built "towns" (fortresses) for all his children. The city was then the site of the Suva Gora monasteries. The monastic people often visited the chifliks, where they were well-housed. The legend says that after the "guests" the settlement was also called Gostivar.

Vrutok

Vrutok, the spring of the largest river in Macedonia, Vardar is in the wider Gostivar surroundings. There, at an altitude of 683 meters, from the base of the mountain Shar rises the river Vardar. The spring of the river Vardar, is one of the greatest natural beauties of the Gostivar region and one of it's kind in Macedonia. From the spring the riverbed of Vardar widens.

.   .   .

Clock Tower

The Clock Tower of Gostivar is an examples of Ottoman architecture of the classical period, built in 1683 by Abu Qebir an Ottoman Bay. By several clocks built into the Clock Tower, it is still in operation and shows the exact time. It is an important monument defining the long cultural heritage of the city.

Bey Mahala Mosque

It is a unique example of the authentic Old Town architecture of the 18th century and is one of the most significant cultural and historical landmarks in the city. The Bey Mahala Mosque was built in 1688. It is also called Clock Mosque because of it's proximity to the Clock Tower.

Cultural Centre ASNOM

The most important place for cultural events in the city is the Cultural Centre ASNOM. During this year, the most important cultural and artistic events are held in this cultural centre.

Kratovo

A small town in North Macedonia, located in the crater of an extinct volcano and known for its bridges and towers.

Where to go, and what to visit?

Lesnovo monastery

Built in the village of Lesnovo, close to the town of Kratovo. Like many other medieval monasteries of Macedonia, it is located up a long and imposing mountain road. It is the largest and best preserved among Byzantine endowments of the 14th century in the Balkans and one the most visually stunning and culturally significant monasteries in Macedonia. The fresco-decoration of Lesnovo Monastery is work of four authors. In regard with wonderfully preserved details and variety of scenes they comprise the horizon of the Byzantine painting and one of the most magnificent artistic achievements at the beginning of the 14th century.

Stone Dolls of Kuklica / Merry Wedding / Drunk Matchmakers

The whole place covers an area of 0.4 km 2 with an altitude of 420 meters. The rocky pyramids and pillars were created between Eocene and Pliocene as a result of a volcanic mass and they are old more than 10 million years.

This bizarre array of stones is said by legend to be a petrified wedding party – formed some 50,000 years ago. Found in Kuklici near the city of Kratovo, one can make out (at a push) the bride, the groom, the best man and the maid of honour.

National Parks

Mavrovo National Park

North Macedonia boasts three national parks, of which Mavrovo is the largest stretching over 192,000 acres from Lake Mavrovo to the Albanian border. It was founded in 1949 and takes in the artificial Lake Mavrovo, as well as the highest mountain peaks in the country, allowing for skiing and snowboarding in the winter. Mavrovo's impressive forests contain more than 100 rare species of trees, and its rugged hilltops are rich in wild herbs and teas that can be easily collected by hand. The best time for skiing in Mavrovo is from

November to April. In the warmer months, The National Park becomes lush and verdant. Lake Mavrovo is the largest artificial lake in the country. In the summer it becomes a popular swimming and boating destination. Many choose to stay in Mavrovo for a couple of days at one of the hotels along the lake shore. One unusual thing about Lake Mavrovo is the submerged St. Nicholas Church. It was purposely flooded in 1953 when the lake was dug, but has since become partially exposed, creating an unexpected sight.

In the Mavrovo national park is located one of the most beautiful monasteries in the country – Sveti Jovan Bigorski (St. John the Baptist). This Byzantine monastery is located on the main road from Gostivar to Debar, two kilometers before the village Rostusa. But it is known for its 19th century masterful colossal wood carvings and stone architecture. The wood carving shows a number of biblical scenes from both the Old and New Testament.

Pelister National Park

Located aside Macedonia's southern borderline with Greece, running along the Baba Mountain (the third-highest in Macedonia), only 15 km (9 m) from North Macedonia's second biggest city Bitola, Pelister is one of the first protected national parks in the Balkans. Due to the relict of the tertiary flora – Molika (Pinus Peuce Griseb), and the morphological and glacial relief in the alpine part of the mountain, in 1948 Pelister was declared a National Park. Making an invigorating natural escape from urban life. Mt. Pelister itself stands magisterially at 2,601 meters high. The park is also rich in springs, streams and rivers, and contains two glacial lakes locally known as the Mountain's Eyes. Pelister is also known for its two mountain lakes, which are called Pelister's Eyes. The Big lake is 2,218 meters above the sea level while the Small lake is 2,180 meters high. Here are the sources of many rivers. The climate in Pelister National Park is diverse. On the peaks, there is snow even in July, and in some places the new snow meets the old from previous years. The beauty of the landscape is enhanced by the diversified wildlife: bears, roe deer, wolves, chamois, deer, wild boars, rabbits, several species of eagles, partridges, redbilled jackdaws, and the endemic Macedonian Pelagonija trout.

Galicica National Park

Situated on Mount Galicica, that is a part of the mountain range of Sara-Pind the park covers an area of 227 km2 between the Lakes of Ohrid and Prespa, and it stretches in a meridian direction. Due to its exceptional natural beauty and extremely opulent and endemic flora and fauna, in 1958 the Macedonian section of the mountain was proclaimed a National Park.In addition to the extraordinary natural beauty and aesthetic values, Galicica is also a unique environment with well-preserved natural flora in several ecosystems. The flora in the National Park Galicica covers more than 800 species, among which there are numerous relict and endemic forms whose farthest limit of distribution is Mount Galicica itself.

The presence of eleven local endemic forms discovered so way is quite remarkable. These forms exist only on the slopes of the Mount Galicica, and are clear evidence of the specific floral structure of the mountain. The fauna on Galicica is also prolific and diverse. There are no precise data about the number of invertebrate species. Vertebrates are present with 170 species: 10 amphibians, 18 reptiles, 124 birds, and 18 mammals.

Krushevo

Located on Bushava Mountain, about 30 km away from Prilep is the home town of one of the most famous singers of all time of the Balkans – Toshe Proeski. Its old architecture and all conditions necessary for pleasant winter holidays, make Krushevo an ideal place for relaxation. Surrounded by impeccable nature, and sensing the altitude even as you breathe in the air, Krushevo is like straight out of a fairytale – a nature parallel to a private resort, if you will. Each year on Ilinden the town wears a festive look: on the balconies and at the windows of all the houses shaggy hand-woven blankets (yambolias – Jambolii) in all kinds of colors are exhibited. This historical city located on 1250 m above the sea level, is only 140 km away from Skopje.

What to visit?

Makedonium (Ilinden Uprising)

Representing the diligent struggle for freedom, it is a place Macedonians feel keen respect towards. It also represents the Ilinden uprising, celebrated on the second of August, when the town witnesses a transformation. Much of the state political elite gather, and the town is filled to capacity and then some.

Meckin Kamen

The one monument that symbolizes the last and desperate attempts of the troop led by Pitu Guli to defend the Republic of Krushevo, the only independent area in the whole of the Ottoman Republic at the time. Death or freedom, are the words carved into the stone.

Tose Proeski Memorial House

Tose Proeski was legendary Macedonian pop singer who tragically died in car accident in 2007. He is beloved in all ex Yugoslav countries.

The building is in the shape of a cross and it was opened on 25 April

2011, and at 870 square meters a large number of photos and 350 exhibits are exposed, which materialize the entire life time of Tose Proeski. Chronologically, the house is divided in six parts: life path, music career, everyday life, Tose as humanist and believer, Tose and his fans and Tose forever. In his memorial house you can see his many personal effects and there is a place to listen to all his famous recordings. You will also see his wax sculpture.

Berovo

A small town near the Maleshevo Mountains, famous for Berovo lake and the forest of the Malesevo Mountains, Berovo craftsmen are well known for their skill in traditional wood crafting and Berovo cheese is their best known specialty. An entirely shrouded lake, set in the middle of a dense pine forest, this place becommes the new definition for the famous slogan "paradise on Earth ". Some of the best honey that you will ever taste, cheese prepared in so many ways, and all the specialties the Maleshevo region has to offer.

Berovo, offering cold summers and relaxing mountainous scenery will charge your batteries and allow you to explore Macedonian tradition and cuisine in a more steady rhythm.

The most famous place in the Maleshevija Region is the Aurora Resort.

Aurora Resort & Spa

Covering 5 hectares of natural scenery 6 km from Berovo, the Aurora Resort & Spa opened in July 2011. It offers fresh mountain air, wellness facilities, and an infinity pool with views of Lake Berovo and the Malesh Mountains.

This eco-friendly property is built with local rock and wood. The

Aurora offers several pools and a stylish restaurant with a terrace. Guests can enjoy the luxurious spa facilities for an additional charge.

Saint Archangel Michael

Other than the lake coast you can visit the beautiful and traditional monastery.

Located on the road to the Berovo lake, it speaks volumes about tradition, religion, and makes for a perfect place to visit.

Getting to Berovo by bicycle

The road from Vinica to Berovo is one of the most scenic trails for cycling, following the Bregalnica river, and decorated with dense forest, beehives along the road, as well as passing through some of the most rustic villages in The Balkans such as Budinarci, a real jewel if you are into rustic villages from the 18th century.

Strumica

As the largest city of the Southeast region, Strumica is its cultural, trade and political center. named after the Strumica River which runs through it, the city has food industry, textile factories and a developed domestic and international trade network. Strumica is full of sights. If one feels like hiking then they should visit the nearby Mountain Belasica and the dazzling waterfalls of Smolare and Koleshino.

Where to stay?

.   .   .

Hotel Ilinden

Situated in the center of Strumica, the hotel offers rooms with free WiFi, a balcony, cable TV, a seating area, and a telephone. The private bathroom comes with a shower or a bath tub. All rooms are air conditioned.

Guests can enjoy breakfast at the property. Ilinden Hotel also offers an à la carte restaurant with a bar. A grocery shop can be reached in a 2-minute walk. A public bus stops 2 km from Hotel Ilinden. Vodocha Lake can be reached in 10 minutes by car.

Villa Park Hotel

It features a garden and a bar in Strumica. Among the facilities of this property are a restaurant, a 24-hour front desk and room service, along with free WiFi. The accommodation provides evening entertainment and a kids' club.

Location: in the center of the city

What to visit?

Bansko Spa

Termo mineral spa in Strumica from ancient times and one of the rare preserved Roman monuments of its kind in Europe, with a capacity of over 50 l/sec. It is located about 12 km east of Strumica, at the foot of the Belasica Mountain. The spa Roman Bath (Therma) had a changing room, sauna, pools with hot and cold water. It probably originates from the 11th century, from the time of the Roman Emperor Caracalla, known for the construction and renewal of baths throughout the Empire.

The whole spa site offers excellent accommodation facilities and conditions for combined tourism types.

Smolare Waterfalls

The Smolare Waterfall located in the immediate vicinity of the village of Smolare, on the mountain Belasica, at an altitude of 600 meters. It is an object with a height of about 35 meters. At the bottom of the waterfall there is a giant pot, the length of which is about five meters in the direction of flowing river water, its width is 11 meters, and the depth is about half a meter. Next to it, there is an access road and an arranged site for visitors with tourist and recreational function.

Kolesino waterfalls

It is located in the lower course of the Baba River at an altitude of 500 meter. It has a height of 15 meters and a width of about six meters. According to the occurrence, it belongs to the tectonic waterfalls. In the immediate vicinity of about 100 meters, there are several smaller waterfalls and slopes arranged in a row with heights of up to five metres.

Monastery St. Leontius, village Vodoca

Filled with monks and church services, the restored lodgings again became a residential complex of the Strumica Diocese. The monastery is located in the village of Vodoca, which received its name according to the terrible event of 1014, when on that place under Belasica14,000 soldiers of Tsar Samuil were blinded by the Byzantines.

Carevi Kuli (King's Towers) over Strumica

The oldest discoveries about the fortress raised on the hill southwest of Strumica speak for life even before the Roman Empire, the pre-historic period until the Middle Ages. According to some archaeologists, those could be remains of the ancient city of Astraion. All the previous findings suggest that on this site there were various civilizations in a period of about seven thousand years. The fortress was built on a leveled plateau on the top of the hill, which steeply rises above Strumica at an altitude of 445 meters, from which it is possible to see the entire Strumica valley.

OHRID

T<small>HE CITY OF THE IMMORTAL</small> O<small>HRID IS THE SUBLIME LAKESIDE POINT</small>
that for many represents the culmination of the North Macedonian

experience, a kingdom of light and water, a repository of ancient ruins from Macedonia's earlier kingdoms. Ohrid's major attractions are all located within a remarkably concentrated and eminently walk-able area, among and above the narrow streets of the Old Town lined with restaurants and cafes perfectly suited for relaxing in the cool summer evenings. Ohrid's many cafe bars and nightclubs also make for a vibrant nightlife. Outside of July and August, the tourist circus subsides and the town becomes more lived in. The uniqueness of Lake Ohrid and the city's historical architecture has been attested by UNESCO, honoring it with an official designation as one of the few places on the cultural institution's list "World Inheritance". The city is known to have 365 churches and monasteries, so you could visit one per day.

Where to stay?

Aleksandrija hotel

The luxury Aleksandrija hotel right on the bank of the scenic Ohrid Lake offers you elegantly furnished rooms with a host of amenities for a pleasant stay in UNESCO-protected surroundings.

Park Golden View Hotel

Located 2.3 km from Port Ohrid in Ohrid, Park Golden View Hotel features a restaurant, bar and free WiFi throughout the property. The hotel has a seasonal outdoor pool and views of the mountain. Free private parking is available on site. You will find a 24-hour front desk at the property. You can play tennis at this hotel, and bike hire is available. The hotel also offers car hire.

Early Christian Basilica is 2.7 km from Park Golden View Hotel, while Saint Sofia is 2.5 km away. The nearest airport is Ohrid Airport, 11 km from the property.

. . .

Villa Milka

Located just a 5-minute walk from Ohrid's town centre, Villa Milka offers rooms with air conditioning, private balconies, flat-screen TV and free Wi-Fi. Milka Villa provides a 24-hour reception, airport transfers and bike rental. There is free private parking and a café bar with terrace where guests can enjoy a refreshing drink.

Ohrid Airport is only a 20-minute drive away and Lake Ohrid is 400 m away.

Hotel Monastery Sveti Stefan

Featuring free WiFi and a sun terrace, Hotel Monastery Sveti Stefan offers accommodation in Ohrid and a 5-minute walk away from the lake. Free private parking is available on site. Guests can relax in the on site garden. The hotel also offers bike hire. Ancient Theatre of Ohrid is 7 km from Hotel Monastery Sveti Stefan and Samoil's Fortress is 7 km from the property. The nearest airport is Ohrid Airport, 15 km from the property.

What to visit?

St. Jovan of Kaneo

St. Jovan of Kaneo was founded at the end of the 13th century and dedicated to St. John the Baptist. Its scenic location and distinctive Byzantine-style architecture make it one of the most photographed places in North Macedonia – from Lake Ohrid and from the shore. The monastery sits perched on a cliff just above the fishing village of Kaneo, overlooking the placid waters of Lake Ohrid. It has become the symbol of Ohrid. You can walk to the church about 15 min. and when coming back to the harbor you can just find one of the little bobbing boats cluster beneath the church. They will take you back for 300MKD - 6 euro.

National workshop for Handmade Paper

Ohrid has been printing paper since the 16th century and this museum-cum-shop has one of only two copies of the Gutenberg Press in the world. The Staff are willing to give a demonstration of the paper-making process, and the teeny museum also sells handmade paper products such as pretty gift bags and notebooks. The view of the water is awesome, you can look through the water and hear the waves crash. Bring some lunch and walk up the hill to have a pick-nick.

Zalivot na koskite

Bay of Bones / Museum on Water is located at the lake of Ohrid. It is an authentic reconstruction of the pile dwelling settlement from around 700 B.C, built on stilts, which you see as part of a cruise on Lake Ohrid to St.Naum. The name Bay of Bones stems from the fact that during the archaeological excavations lots of animal bones were found.

Plaoshnik, St. Clement Church (Church of Sveti Kliment i Pantelejmon)

Saluting the lake from Ohrid's hilltop, Plaoshnik is home to the multidomed medieval Church of Sveti Kliment i Pantelejmon, the foundations of a 5th-century basilica and a garden of intricate early Christian flora-and-fauna mosaics.

The St. Clement Church is originally constructed in the 13th century and known as the St. Panteleimon Church, it housed the relics of St. Clement. It was converted into a mosque in the 15th century during the Ottoman period before being reconstructed in the 16th century and turned back into a church. A visit to St. Clement Church will reveal medieval frescoes, early Christian mosaics, and Byzantine-style architecture that is common throughout the Balkans.

Kukjata na Robevci (Robevci's House, Ohrid's National Museum)

Located in the Old Town, this beautiful museum house belonged to one of the richest people in Ohrid.

The museum costs MKD 150 to enter, build in old style of ottoman house. I would highly recommend a visit as all the floors are accessible now. On the ground floor there is an interesting exhibition of local modern art; on the first, rooms preserving items belonging to the Robevci family who used to live there; on the second, archaeological exhibit and on the top floor a large room with impressive Ohrid wood carving.

Samuilova Tvrdina (fortress)

When Tsar Samuil moved the capital of the Empire to Ohrid, he built one of the greatest strongholds in the Balkans. Today, Tsar Samuil's Fortress is a popular vantage point for spectacular views of the city of Ohrid and Ohrid Lake. Admission to the fortress is just 30 MKD.

Ancient Theatre of Ohrid

Near the Center of Ohrid is the Ancient Theatre – an open-air Hellenistic-style theatre that was built around 200 B.C. with a capacity of 4,000 spectators. During Roman times it was used for gladiatorial battles for executing Christians, leading to its abandonment after the fall of the Roman Empire. Nowadays, it is used as a stage during the annual Ohrid Summer Festival, Ohrid Calling.

North Macedonian countryside

Rural tourism in Macedonia focuses on participating in a rural lifestyle (subcategory of ecotourism). Rural tourism exists in Macedonia provides the travelers accommodation in a scenic location ideal for rest and relaxation.

Elsani village, Ohrid

Located between the green heights of Mount Galicica and the blue waters of Lake Ohrid, Elsani is a vibrant village whose inhabitants of all generations are enjoying the comforts of the 21st century, still surrounded by the smell of home made bread, brandy, wine, and traditions that never fade. The nearest restaurants are located outside the village, by the lakeside.

From early April to late October, the days are long with many sunny hours and medium air temperatures, between 20° and 30° C. This is the right time for outdoor activities, such as water sports and mountain hiking.

Trpejca village, Ohrid

Due to the its setting between the rocks this small fishing village has managed to preserve its charm and escape the overgrow of tourism, which is way is offered referred as Saint Tropez of Macedonia. Trpejca has a great long but narrow beach with the cleanest waters on the lake. If you want a bit more privacy on the beach you can arrange with one of the many locals who own boat and be taken to a one of the isolated beaches around the village. Of course the boat will come back for you at the time you arrange, this usually costs between 200 MKD and 500 MKD ($4-$9 / 3 euro – 8 euro).

Vevchani, Struga

The village of Vevchani high in the hills to the north of Lake Ohrid is famous for its springs, its appeal to artists – and for the fact that briefly following the break-up of Yugoslavia it declared itself the independent Republic of Vevchani. The village – population 2,500, still likes to think of itself as a separate entity, with its own passports and currency. And if you drink enough Vevchani wine, you can become an honorary citizen.

Radozda village, Struga

Better known as *the rare coastal jewel of Macedonia*. The 10 centuries old Radozda is a place that leaves people breathless, returns the calmness and the ability to become one with the nature. Furthermore it will bring smile on your face due to the hospitality offered by the local people. The centuries – old receipts that are still being prepared in this beautiful place, will be a holiday to your stomach.

Gorna Belica village, Struga

This almost abandoned village is a paradise on Earth, it can be reached by driving, biking or walking from Struga, or by hiking from Vevcani. If you want to fully experience the life of the locals you can find accommodation in some of the cottages of the villagers who have migrated. If not there is a modern hotel in the village's center.

Galicnik village, Debar

The village with extraordinary traditional architecture is located about 10 km from the artificial lake of Mavrovo, deep in the Mavrovo national park. Galicnik is famous for the Galicka Svadba, a traditional and public summer wedding, held annually on the day of the village feast of the Patron Saint Petrovden. During the wedding, local men will dance the Teskoto oro, a national dance who symbolizes the overcoming of the difficult moments in life.

There are two specialties you have to try if you visit this village – mature yellow cheese known as kaskaval, as well as the local white cheese known as belo sirenje. Every summer there is a Summer Art Colony being organized in the amphitheater in the village's center.

DOJRAN

A HISTORIC CITY IN THE SOUTHEASTERN PART OF THE REPUBLIC OF Macedonia on the shores of Dojran Lake.

Besides the Lake on the Macedonian side, there are three settlements: Nov and Star Dojran and Nikolic with more than 4000 inhabitants. Star Dojran is a settlement on the western part of the Lake. Today the settlement has a tourist-recreational function with a number of holiday homes. Along the coast there are 40 hotels and other accommodation facilities, several modern casinos and over 600 weekend cottages.

The legend about the city's name

A very beautiful girl named Dojrana lived in the settlement. An Ottonman bey fell in love with her and asked her parents to give their blessing for her to be his wife even though Dojrana did not love him. One day she went to fill the jars with water from a spring, the bey noticed her and ran towards her. Running Dojrana threw herself into the spring for the next morning the spring to expand and flood the whole place becoming a lake. After the name of the beautiful girl, the lake received the name Dojransko, and the settlement Dojran.

Where to stay?

Apartments and Villas Janev

Set in Star Dojran, 30 km from Gevgelija, Apartments and Villas Janev offers a garden and free WiFi. Strumica is 40 km from Apartments and Villas Janev, while Kerkíni is 48 km away.

Villa Gloria

Boasting a garden and a terrace, Villa Gloria offers accommodation in Star Dojran with free WiFi and garden views. The air-conditioned accommodation is 31 km from Gevgelija. Speaking English, Italian and Serbian at the reception, staff are always on hand to help.

Strumica is 40 km from the villa, while Kerkíni is 47 km from the property.

GEVGELIJA

THE SUN-DRENCHED GEVGELIJA, IS LOCATED ONLY A FEW KILOMETERS above the Greek border. Having several hotel chains that promote casino entertainment in the region for which Gevgelija is best known.

What to visit?

The Town Museum

A town which has long history and rich culture must possess a place where evidences and examples of the rich history will be preserved and displayed. Gevgelija is a beautiful town with many significant buildings and places that need to be seen. The Museum of Gevgelija is one of them and you will not regret that visit ever.

The Museum is located on the well-known street Marshal Tito, which connects the Central Square with the Railway Station. It was built in 1906 and it is an example of beautiful architectural style which is still preserved today.

National Museum of Gevgelija

The museum is housed in an adaptive building, which was built in 1900. It has an extensive and specific architectural collection, which numbers several thousand museum objects. Some representative exhibits are on display in the permanent archaeological exhibition "Vardar hill with surrounding sites". The exhibition contains about 350 objects dating from the epochs of the Neolithic to the Roman period from the end of 2nd to 4th century AD. The city of Gevgelija is located in the heart of prehistoric and ancient Paeonia Amfaksitida area with its central settlement Gortinija

Negorski Banji(Spa)

A modern tourist and health center for prolonged treatment and rehabilitation of patients in modern facilities set for all types of therapy in the field of physical medicine and rehabilitation.

The complex is located at 3 kilometers from Gevgelija, at an altitude of 50 meters. It is located in a very specific environment at the foot of Mount Kozuf, between rich and rare clear forest, which forms a natural park. The Ash tree forest covers an area of 22 hectares around the complex Negorski Banji. The spa complex Negorski Banji offers accommodation in 3 hotels.

Resort Smrdliva Voda

North Macedonia offers a unique opportunity to take you thousands of years back in time and enjoy the benefits of the mineral and thermomineral waters that spring out from almost every inch of land. The mix of the modern spa complexes and the remains of the once Roman and Turkish baths offer a one-time feeling.

Famous for its sulfur baths and water used for healing gastric and kidney diseases, the resort is located about 24 km from Gevgelija. This spa complex is fully outfitted with 400 villas, a hotel, sports center and ski slopes.

Where to stay?

Apollonia Hotel & Casino

Located in the very center of the city, this has been the place for gambling for the last 30 years. If you're looking for luxury accommodation, great excitement with plenty of choices from live games or slots and an always warm and welcoming five star service then you should definitely head over and experience the thrill of Apollonia. The casino is open 24/7 and offers free drinks and buffet for playing guests paired with various entertainment and many lottery prizes. The hotel part features several types of rooms, all luxuriously furbished and fully equipped, as well as a lounge bar, garden cafe and in-house restaurant.

Ramada Plaza

The luxurious 5-star hotel, situated near Macedonian – Greek border, features a grandiose Princess Casino, 2 restaurants, a gym and a spa. Located 45 km from Thessaloniki and 160 km from Skopje, the hotel stretches on over 4000 square meters.

Elegantly decorated, spacious and luxurious, all rooms feature free Wi-Fi, LCD TV with satellite channels and a comfortable seating area. A tea and a coffee maker are provided.

Hotel Ramada Plaza have Artemis restaurant, offering culinary delights from around the world. Powerful spotlights and the open bar of a night club Next provide a memorable clubbing experience

A sauna and a hot tub, a chic indoor pool and massage rooms invite you to enjoy and relax.

PRILEP

THIS CITY IS KNOWN AS "THE CITY BENEATH MARKO'S TOWERS" because of its proximity to the towers of the legendary hero, King Marko.

The legend about the city's name

There are several assumptions about the origin of the name. According to a legend by Marko Cepenkov, the people who started to move there, built their houses next to Marko's fortress, and due to the attached houses (prilepeni) it was named Prilep. In the same legend, it was mentioned that it was a prilebno mesto (a place where bread was made). According to some researchers, the name has an Old Slavic origin, meaning a muddy, swampy place, a place beside the mud. According to Blaze Koneski, the name is derived from the personal names Prilepa and Prilepka, which are preserved in Russian anthroponymy. The settlements in the wider region date from antiquity, such as the archeological site Stibera, near the village of Cepigovo. Traces of prehistoric settlement were discovered near Marko's Towers.

Where to stay?

Apartment in Prilep

Situated in Prilep, 41 km from Bitola, Apartment in Prilep features a garden and free WiFi.

Guests at the apartment can enjoy a continental breakfast. The apartment in Prilep offers a barbecue. Also a casino is available on site and both hiking and cycling can be enjoyed within close proximity of the accommodation.

Atlas City Center Hotel

Set in Prilep, Atlas City Center Hotel offers 4-star accommodation with a bar. Among the facilities of this property are a restaurant, a 24-hour front desk and room service, along with free WiFi.

Continental and à la carte breakfast options are available every morning at the hotel.

The area is popular for cycling, and bike hire and car hire are available at Atlas City Center Hotel.

The accommodation provides an ironing service, as well as business facilities like fax and photocopying.

What to visit?

- **Monastery Treskavec (St. Bogorodica)**

Built in the 12th century and located in one of the most remote and inaccessible places in the country - on the rocky Mount Zlatovrv, only 8 km north of Prilep, it currently has only one monk. The monastery possesses a large collection of Byzantine frescoes and that is the main reason why it is visited, apart from the peaceful environment you can find there.

- **Markovi Kuli (Marko's Towers)**

Situated to the northwest of Prilep, above the village of Varosh the towers are named after the Macedonian prince Marko Mrnjavčević from medieval times. The ruins are easily reachable on foot from the town within 30 minutes. Views are great and on the top of the will there is a large cross. The rampart on this terrain dates from the 13th and 14th centuries and is in good condition. The walls are about one meter thick and were built of limestone mortar and rest upon the large limestone rocks.

- **Prilep Lake**
- **Prilep's Old Bazaar**

Located in the center of the town with extremely low prices in this place you can find everything from clothes to vegetables, fruits and meat. And the fresh groceries are mostly organic. Macedonians call the place the Pazar not bazaar. So make sure you ask for directions to the pazar instead of the directions of the bazaar.

You will be pleasantly surprised by the variety of shops, coffee bars and restaurants on offer, but yet the real old fashioned feel to the place.

- **Mound of the Unbeaten**

A World War II memorial in the Park of the Revolution, built in 1961 in honor to the martyrs and fallen fighters of the People's Liberation Struggle in Macedonia.

WINERIES

Popova Kula Winery, Demir Kapija

The Popova Kula Winery was built to produce the highest quality Macedonian wine and offer quality wine tourism in the region. By using regional best grapes in combination with latest sophisticated technology and the experience of the team of expert wine makers, The Popova Kula Winery has succeeded in creating wines that are proud of. No one can resist the unique architectural beauty of the winery, as well as unique aroma and gentle taste of the wines. The Popova Kula Hotel offers unique experience to its guests with its distinct 4 suites and 7 rooms each decorated separately to represent our 7 types of wines.

Winery Tikves, Kavadarci

As early as in Roman times, a tradition in Macedonia was flourishing - a tradition to craft enchantingly powerful wines exhibiting the scent of the south, having a symphonic flavour and epitomizing the joyfulness of Macedonians. Tikveš Winery is one of the most important creators of this tradition. For more than 125 years, the sky, land, sun and vineyards in the south of Europe, each with its own share, have been a part of the story about Tikveš wines. Tikveš Winery has been crafting and aging premium Macedonian wines ... ever since 1885.

At the late 70's of the 20th century aggro-combine Tikveš is founded by merging several smaller agricultural cooperatives. Tikveš becomes the largest winery in Southeast Europe.

At 1973 the wine T'ga za jug, in honor of Struga Poetry Evenings, is crafted. A star is born.

WINERY TIKVES produces 24 types of wine, out of which the most attractive are: T'ga za jug, Traminec, Kratoshija, Chardonay, Alexandria – Cabernet Sauvignon and Alexandria – Riesling, and the famous Tikveš grape brandy – Lozova rakija – Zolta.

At the Wine Innovation Forum in Paris – 2008, Tikveš Winery is ranked among the world's 30 most innovative wine brands.

FESTIVALS AND EVENTS IN NORTH MACEDONIA

STRUMICA CARNIVAL

An annual carnival held in Strumica. It is one of the most important customs and traditions of its kind in Macedonia. The carnival went perhaps farther in its transformation than all traditional masking games, both due to the time when it takes place and its purpose and function. The Strumica Carnival is held traditionally every year within the trimer days, that is, at the beginning of the great Easter fasting.

Each participant chooses their own theme and idea of masking, while group masks represent a common idea for the whole group. Among the types of masks, the most common are the anthropomorphic ones and there are also zoomorphic and zoo anthropomorphic masks. The number of participants in the carnival in Strumica, as well as the number of visitors, increases every year, and besides the local participants, guests from abroad regularly participate.

Vevcani Caranival

One of the most famous village festivals held in the Balkans is the Vevcani Carnival. It is believed that the custom is over 1,400 years old. It is based on old Pagan beliefs and rituals. Essentially the Carnival is the ritual of calling after Saint Basil the Great, which coincides with the Twelve Days of Orthodox Christmas and the Orthodox New Year. The festivity is dedicated to Saint Basil the Great. Traditionally, this year from 12th to 14th January will be held Vevcani Carnival which is one of the oldest cultural events in Macedonia, which traditionally celebrates the arrival of the New Year according to the old calendar. The participants of the Carnival are known as "Vasiličari". Vevcani Carnival as an event unites all forms of expression of our traditional culture, transforming the needs of contemporary society, treating topics from today. The annual carnival is a mix of pagan customs translated into modern language. In 1993 the Carnival and the village of Vevcani officially became apart of the World Federation of Carnival Cities. In recent years a special "Carnival Passport" has been issued at the Carnival. The Vevcani Carnival, which claims a 14 century long legacy, is held every year from 13 to 14 January in the southwestern Macedonian village of Vevcani.

Ohrid Calling

Every year Avalon Production organizes a 4- day festival with a line-up of 13 – 16 artists in Ohrid. Every year there are a minimum of 20.000 visitors per day, not only from North Macedonia, but Europe as well.

D Festival

Established in 2011 and raised by the idea of having a unique open-air music event that will offer an alternative for satisfying the need for a summer festival at the authentic and outstanding Dojran coast – "D FESTIVAL" has already confirmed and justified its initiative in the best way. It is a young festival which is always held in a perfect atmosphere that constantly leads to euphoria and represents a unique evening drive on positive energy, contributed by the thousands of fans and the finest artists of the local, regional and world music scene.

The first go green festival in the country. The Go Green together with interested visitors patroled the festival village and made sure to raise awareness about the use of less waste for one use and the need for the waste to be appropriately delayed marked places. Each year D Festival is the party destination for more than 8.000 visitors who have enjoyed this festival with the remarkable concert performances of the music artists like Stereo MC's, Sonique, Djaikovski, Dubioza Kolektiv, Bernays Propaganda, String Forces, Superhiks, AREA, S.A.R.S., Baildsa, Zijan and many more. Everybody is eager for the upcoming edition of the festival. The date of the festival (end of July) is also a season which every year attracts more and more international and local tourists and many young people who believe in the potential of Dojran as attractive location.

Where to stay?

The campsite is the best way to feel and live the real festival atmosphere of D FESTIVAL: let the sun wake you, be close as possible to the festival site, enjoy the Dojran Lake and the beautiful beach located next to the campsite, make new friends and party with the thousands of young festival visitors!

D Festival's campers have access to drinkable water, showers, wireless internet, food and drinks stores, beach and various options such (lockers for personal items, recharge-spot for mobile phones etc.). During their stay in the camp, the camp visitors can enjoy all stages and they can take part in different workshops, debates, games, recreation and many other interesting activities.

. . .

Traksirat Festival

Showcasing a multifarious blend of bands and musicians from a number of musical genres, the festival is a beacon of musical diversity that prides itself on being an international and universal music event. With thousands of revellers cramming into packed arenas, this event is North Macedonia's equivalent of Glastonbury or T in the Park, and past performers have included The Kaiser Chiefs and Iggy Pop. Taking place in Skopje, the festival is easily accessible from the city. Taskirat takes place at the end of November every year and stretches over a one week period, so guests can attend for one day, or choose to stay for the whole event.

The Manaki Brothers Film Festival

Proudly one of the world's oldest film festivals, and celebrates the work of cinematographers from around the globe. Established in 1979, this exciting event was inspired by Yanaki and Milton Manaki, the Macedonian brothers who pioneered 20th century film making in the Balkans with their documentaries and photographic art, some of which was made as early as 1904. Premiering films from a variety of genres, from short film to animation, the festival is a celebration of all things film, and aims to showcase the creative works of cinematographers both young and old, local and international. Set in the beautiful city of Bitola, an area of some fascinating ancient architecture, the Manaki Brothers Festival takes place every September.

Strumica Open Festival

With four separate stages showcasing a range of artists and musical styles, from folk and pop-rock to progressive house, music lovers are

86

well catered for here and can find an artist for every one of their moods during the 10 day festival.

OUTDOOR ACTIVITIES

PARAGLIDING – SEE NORTH MACEDONIA FROM THE TOP

Macedonia is truly an amazing country for adventure sports. The mountainous region in Skopje and Mavrovo, the beautiful view upon Ohrid Lake and the rocky region in Prilep will for sure take your breath away. Macedonia has several professional paragliding clubs where you can get full equipment and professional guides for this sport. Don't miss the chance to fly over Macedonia, with or without experience, we can take you to your paragliding ride for ultimate enjoyment. Paragliding as a recreational and competitive adventure sport of flying para – gliders is widespread all over the country. These regions have amazing landscapes that are certainly worth to be seen. No experience is necessary.

Tandem flights are the easiest, fastest and safest way to experience paragliding for the first time. If you can ran 2-3 meters, you can fly with us! After a ten minute briefing our professional tandem pilot will take you into the air for a flight that lasts from 20 – 40 minutes depending on flying conditions. The passenger (you) and the flight instructor each have their own comfortable harness. You are then connected together and finally connected to the glider. Two minutes later, you're airborne! Once in the air your flight instructor will explain to you what he is doing and how para – gliders fly. If conditions permit, you may be offered hands on control of the glider.

FLYING ADVENTURE PROGRAMS

Fly Over Ohrid Lake

1700 m ASL

Take off is in Galichica mountain.

During the flight you can see Ohrid City and all lake side (Peshtani, Trpejca, St Naum).

This flying adventures is approx. 2h.

Flight time is approx. 15-20 min, depending of thermal condition.

Price: 69 €

The price includes: Transport from your Hotel to the take of place and back, Photos and Videos direct uploaded in One Drive, you get link from your flight files...

Fly Over Ohrid

1100m / 1350 m ASL

Flying take off is from Galichica mountain.

During flight you can see City of Ohrid and first side of Ohrid beach.

This flying adventure is approx. 1h.

Flight time is approx. 10-15 min, depending of thermal condition.

The price includes: Transport from your Hotel to the take of place and back, Photos and Videos direct uploaded in One Drive, you get link from your flight files.

Fly Over Ohrid Lake

ACROBATIC / or Flight with heart

Flight for Adrenalin, strait from the 1700 m ASL in Galichica take off point.

After first thermal point we lifting up near to top of the mountain Galichica highest point (Magaro)

During flight you can see all side area Ohrid lake, Macedonia, and Albania Side.

Price: 89€

The price includes: Transport from your Hotel to the take of place and back, Photos and Videos direct uploaded in One Drive, you get link from your flight files...

Entry fee of 5 euro for National park is not included in the price...

Horse riding

In North Macedonia it would not be extraordinarily to see horse being used as a mean of transportation, however, only in the mountainous villages. Besides that, mostly, the horses are being used as a tourist attraction. Horse riding offers benefits beyond simple enjoyment; physically, mentally and emotionally and in our country this will certainly be a very different way to experience the nature and the irreplaceable beauties that have disappeared under the conquest of "civilization" of our time.

KK (Konjacki klub) / Horse club Bistra-Galicnik.

KK Bistra dates back since May 2010. It is a previous reconstruction of KK Medenica which was also governing the district of Bistra Galicnik. With the new structure, ideas and members KK Bistra- Galicnik has really broad spectrum of goals and tasks. The main and most important goal is the development of one type of active tourism in the country of Macedonia. Because of that KK Bistra Galicnik has prepared competent tourist offer which is very interesting for the ones that have certain knowledge of this sport as well as for the beginners, or the ones that come across with this kind of sport for the first time in their lives. However, in this area of active tourism the purpose is having an experience which is actually impossible to feel unless we are not on horse back riding among beautiful nature.

Holiday on a horseback offers a firsthand experience of the riches of Mavrovo National Park. This particular holiday is a great way to discover the beautiful countryside far from the clutter of the urban life. Join us and visit places with beautiful scenery, mighty mountains, crystal clear rivers and waterfalls, smooth and vast green highlands. Lodging in old villages, enjoy the taste of domestic food products offered in the local sheepfolds, sometimes by the fire or sometimes simply in the nature, sitting on a rock in the middle of a pasture taking pleasure in the splendors of life and nature.

Scuba diving – Dive in the mysterious waters of North Macedonia

Lake Ohrid has a dramatic drop-off at its tectonic shelf, which is worth exploring, and there is also a Neolithic stilt village which can be accessed with special permission. In Lake Ohrid, also known as a fresh-water sea, very attractive are the endemic forms of life, such as the Ohrid round sponge living at the depth of 35 meters, the number of underwater pre – historical settlements and the fish in the rocky parts from Gradiste to Trpejca.

Learn to dive in a simple and interesting way following the program and standards of Scuba Schools International and acquire internationally recognized certificate for diving.

Mountain Biking – The real feel

Mountain biking is a great sport to practice in North Macedonia, with more than thousands of off-road and dirt tracks. Each mountain club rents out bicycles and organizes regional mountain-bike tour and smaller local tours. As a clubs they also promote developing biking trails in Macedonia as well as local sustainable tourism to historical and natural sites of interest. North Macedonian mountain bike routes are very good. Bearing in mind that 50% of your country is mountainous, you can consider it perfect for this sport. The routes in Mavrovo are very good and those from Vodno to Matka are perfect! The real excitement in mountain biking is the fact that there are ups and downs from the starting till the ending point, and the very narrow paths so that only one biker can ride through it. And when you add all the curves, then you have real fun.

Sailing

Being available in North Macedonia on the Ohrid Lake and Prespa Lake, sailing as a recreational activity and relaxing water sport is also very popular in the country. The local sailing clubs will make your sailing trip in North Macedonia unforgettable. The fans of this sport can get enormous amusement by sailing through the Macedonian lakes, enjoying both pleasures, of the sport and of the nature.

Kayaking and Canoeing

Kayaking as a sport is very popular in Macedonia especially on the Canyon Matka as a whitewater kayaking, also at the famous Macedonian lakes – Ohrid Lake and Prespa Lake, where you can do kayaking on backwater. Matka is a canyon located west of Skopje, Macedonia. Covering roughly 5,000 hectares, Matka is one of the most popular outdoor destinations in Macedonia and is home to several medieval monasteries. Also, Macedonia offers numerous white-water rapids and a number of competition courses including those on the River Vardar in Skopje itself and at Lake Matka just outside Skopje.

Ski and Snowboard

North Macedonia's ski and snowboard resorts can offer fine snow and mountain challenges for every taste, from beginners to professionals. The ski resorts in Macedonia are hosts of several ski and snowboards cups that atrract visitors from all the world to enjoy the magnificent mountains of snow in Macedonia.

About Mavrovo Ski Center

The Ski center Mavrovo has three chair lifts and eleven ski lifts. The length of chair lifts is 4.800 m. with a capacity of 1.900 persons per hour. With these lifts, skiing is possible from 1.255 m. to 1.860 m. above sea level. The length of the ski lifts is 5.700 m. with a capacity of 10.100 skiers per hour. There are tracks for beginners, advanced and top competitors in the alpine and Nordic categories. The average snow cover is 70 cm. which makes skiing possible, as well as other snow games from November to April.

About Popova Sapka Ski Center

The well-known ski resort Popova Sapka lies above Tetovo in the Shar Mountain. It is well linked to the town by road and a cable railway.

The ski track on the south side of the Shar Mountain is located at 1875 m altitude, 18km from Tetovo and 48 km from Skopje. The gondola chairlift Tetovo- Popova sapka is 7 km long (the ride takes about 40 min). It has a total of 11 chairlifts with a total length of 7,7 km which connect the ski terrains at latitude of 1100 to 2500 m. The total length is 20 km and 3 of those 20 are according to the FIS criteria. (FIS- International Ski Federation).

About Kozuf Ski Resort

Kozuf mountain is a mountain situated in the southern part of the Republic of Macedonia and partly in Greece. Its highest peak is Zelenbeg, at 2171 meters above the sea level. A new and modern ski center was built recently on the mountain. Kozuf is a ski resort with three ski lifts (1 chair lift, 2 surface lifts) and it boast a very impressive 573 meters of vertical descent. Kozuf has 1110 acres of terrain over 12 pistes. Kozuf is best suited to advanced and intermediate skiers and snowboarders. The resort is in its investment phase, working on the platform for developing Kozuf to be a competitive ski resort in the region.

About Krusevo Ski Resort

Situated at an altitude of 1,330 meters above the sea level, Krushevo is the highest town not only in the Republic of North Macedonia, but also in the Balkans. It is a well-known winter ski center and a health resort. The ski terrains are located in the vicinity of the city and the chair lift departures from the very city center. The terrains are located on 1400 m altitude. The ski lifts and chair lifts include: Double chair lift with a capacity of 720 skiers per hour, ski lift anchor with a capacity of 700 skiers per hour, single ski lifts for 600 skiers per hour and baby ski lifts with a capacity of 300 children per hour.

About Pelister Ski Resort

Pelister of North Macedonia is a tiny ski resort with just two ski lifts but it does boast a very impressive 1172 meters of vertical descent. Pelister has 2 pistes and is best suited to advanced and intermediate skiers and snowboarders.

NORTH MACEDONIAN CUISINE

THE NORTH MACEDONIAN CUISINE, OWING TO ITS GEOGRAPHICAL
position, is inspired by Mediterranean, Turkish, and to a lesser extent,
Italian, German and Eastern European. Tavche gravche, a multi-
beaned stew, is seen as the national dish, while mastika, a liqueur
seasoned with mastic, otherwise known as Arabic gum is its national
drink. Macedonians eat a lot of meat. They are also known for their
refreshing heaping salads of fresh greens, tomatoes, and peppers
topped with local cheese. Another popular national drink is the rakia,
usually a very potent alcohol drink that you should drink in very small
quantities. Better known as the North Macedonian brandy comes
under the category of natural medicine, a secretly popular weapon
against many diseases, together with olive oil, garlic, honey and other
local products. For stomach aches, colds, flu and similar illnesses, they
say there is no better medicine than rakija. It will destroy all bacteria
and viruses. Also recommended for muscle pain, not to mention for
disinfection of wounds. Usually, drank as an aperitif, for a morning
wake-up, with cheese and prosciutto, before and after lunch, facilitates
sleep, to forget or to cheer. However, they say that who doesn't drink
homemade rakia, hasn't been drinking rakia at all!

.   .   .

In addition I will present you with some of the most delicious meals of this cuisine.

Sarma

A typical 'winter' dish to warm up is the cabbage rolls with meat & rice named **Sarma**. This is the ultimate comfort food and absolutely everyone eats this. The rolls are made of fermented cabbage leaves and inside there is ground beef and rice – all of this is baked in the oven. There is also a vegetarian version with just rice, and a 'summer' version of the Sarma, made of vine leaves and served with dairy sour cream (sheep, cow or goat's milk). A perfect starter dish, main meal or even snack in between when you're extra hungry.

Pastrmajlija / Samun

Another unique dish is the Pastrmajlija or so called Samun. Depending on where are you located the name of this dish can vary. Well you should ask your self what makes this dish so special, the perfect combination of nice homemade dough in oval shape with pork fat and meat all over the dough, you can chose with what kind of meat your Pastrmajlija / Samun will be made with. Your choices are between pork, white (chicken) meat or s'zdrma (mutton), I personally prefer the mutton because it definitely adds even more unique taste to the existing one. The fat melts over the meat and dough as they bake and makes them incredibly tender and soft. Often, there is an egg too, sunny-side up. Most people eat Pastrmajlija / Samun with 'feferonki' or small, green, fermented hot peppers.

Turli Tava (mixed veggies and meat in a pan)

Vegetarians or not, this dish is super-versatile, tasty, refreshing, filling and comforting. It's as if a whole garden of organic veggies was combined in one pot. There are slices and chunks of peppers, paprika, potatoes, tomatoes, eggplant, okras, courgette slices, onions, garlic, carrots – and if it's a meat version, with beef or pork meat pieces. It can be eaten with or without bread, but this dish is full blown, 100% nutritious and delicious.

Gjomleze

This pie originates from the southwestern part of Macedonia. It is a big soft white pie with a crispy crust. It is still prepared in the same way as hundreds of years ago; with a traditional cooking apparatus called a "sach" Be prepared to spend several hours for this specialty, but it's definitely worth it!

Burek (crispy stuffed pie)

Burek is the best pastry in the world! It's made of pastries filled with ground meat, cheese or spinach and it's found in the cuisines of all Balkan countries that used to be part of the Ottoman Empire.

Kebapi (sausage)

A receipt of grilled minced meat composed into the shape of a sausage. Onions, vegeta (which is a very popular mixture of Macedonian herbs) and bukovec (paprika) are what give this dish its savory flavor.

Kifli

Rolled into the shape of a croissant, kifli are rolls made from yeast and sprinkled with sesame seeds. Kifli are typically either filled with feta cheese or a sweet jam and topped with confectioner's sugar.

Teleska Corba

Meat stew is a traditional dish in Macedonia. Veal stew, tripe stew and chicken stew (and somewhere and fish stew) are served in every restaurant every day from morning till afternoon, usually combined with garlic sauce (makalo) and fresh bread.

Sirenje pod kapak / Sirenje vo furna (Cheese in oven)

Melted cheese or cheese in oven is a delicious North Macedonian specialty, which pizzerias and restaurants usually serve with nicely roasted crispy bread sprinkled with sesame seeds. Cheese in oven is combination of 2-3 different cheeses. If desired, mushrooms, bacon or other dried meat can be added for richer taste.

Zelnik (Pie)

Perfect pie-dish made of dough that is semi-crispy after baking, stuffed with chopped cabbage, or meat, white cheese (feta cheese), chopped leeks or spinach, with a scrambled egg to make a nice firm mixture between the dough layers. It pairs perfectly with a glass of yogurt, a bowl of sour cream or some extra chunks of cheese.

Ajvar / Ajver

This traditional dish which marks the beginning of fall/winter season has been one of North Macedonian's favorites for decades if not even centuries. It is made principally from red bell peppers and oil. Known as the ideal companion to cold winters, it's a food that has no adequate replacement, and in combination with cheese creates irreplaceable and unique pleasure in your mouth.

Ekleri

A pastry made with eggs, which after baked are being filled with a delicious cream made with milk, vanilla, eggs and flour. When cooled are topped with melted chocolate. Many pastry shops made this specialty and in every single one of them you will find a different taste as the receipt can vary.

AFTERWORD

North Macedonia is a great place to visit, most of all because of the unique culture and the way the people live. Our suggestion would be – while you are staying here to try and live all the things and places like the locals because that is the only way to truly get to know a country. The country at first may look small, but it is so rich of nature and has many unexplored places so you will feel like you are a Columbo of the modern times. You will fall in love with North Macedonia from the first minute you get in the country, so with a great sadness in your heart you will say goodbye when you will be leaving.